MIRACLES

of

Simple People

Tabor Hermon

ISBN 978-1-64028-425-8 (Paperback)
ISBN 978-1-64028-426-5 (Digital)

Christian Faith Publishing, Inc.
296 Chestnut Street
Meadville, PA 16335
www.christianfaithpublishing.com

Printed in the United States of America

Contents

Introduction

Disclaimer: I do not believe myself to be better than anyone. I know nothing, and I am sure of it physically not spiritually. All pride separates us from *God*. I am a sixty-year-old male in San Antonio, Texas. All of the stories are true, to the best of my knowledge. I did not pay for miracles. That would have guaranteed made-up stories. Many people cried when sharing their story. It is personal, yet inspiring. Of course, this is a way to share without reproach. God is my witness.

The obvious question is, "What is a miracle?" It cannot be explained—a question with which we all struggle. It is a sign and wonder from God. Science and spirituality need not be antagonistic. Who could deny that we live in a scientific world? A miracle does not come from logic or reason. Things in this world always do. It happens in our physical world. Not in the spiritual world. Miracles are not all divine. A perfect example is the staff turning into a serpent for Moses and Aaron; it was a divine miracle. The staff of the magicians of Pharaoh turning into a serpent was not a divine miracle although it was from a divine source to create doubt. The power of prayer is incredible. Jesus performed nothing but divine miracles. It is spiritual in nature, yet physical in operation. Just being born is a miracle. (Who is not?) While a miracle will increase faith, it will not save any person.

One example is the parting of the Red Sea. That is a major miracle. Walking on water is certainly a major miracle. Water is life, there is none without it. The understanding of life is in living a life of love. There is none to compare to these. These are Bible miracles.

While I firmly believe these happened, there is not anything like that today. The scope of this book does not include spiritual beliefs. We are all free to believe or not believe, if we choose. There is a reason for everything. Testimonies are also miracles. These happen frequently in modern times. While miracles compel a person to belief, they do not incorporate freedom. To have a miracle happen is not a way to believe. We are all capable of believing what we see; conversely, we are all capable of believing what we do not see. True freedom comes from man's will. Please understand when I say man, I am referring to mankind.

Any love, good or bad, comes from the will. It is through freedom that we are saved. We all have freewill. Some believe that getting what you want is freedom. The only true freedom comes from God. That is genuine freedom. Faith is belief. Saving faith is only achieved from our love toward God and love toward the neighbor as self. We should do all for the neighbor what we would do for ourselves. That is selfless, not selfish. It is easier said than done, yet we all can do it. There is no true faith without love. Some miracles are listening to that voice inside you. People disappear as well as tumors. It happens way more frequently than we think.

Just waking up is a miracle, albeit not a major miracle to us. Nothing is a given. Miracles can seem like fiction; however, they are not. Sometimes truth is stranger than fiction. We all believe what we see and hear. Miracles cannot be seen or heard. A person must believe what they cannot see to believe in miracles. They happen today, just as in ancient times. Actually, we all experience miracles on a regular basis. Nothing happens without a reason. Taking anything for granted is easy to do. We can be blinded to miracles. Relying on our self-guidance causes many things to be missed. What we see spiritually is the key. Love toward all will open our eyes. It is not what you see but what you do. Whether physical or spiritual, it is the same. Life and all its details are a miracle. Love is the key. The more we love and are in a state of gratitude, the closer we are to God.

We go to God, and God comes to us. We must shun all that separates us from God. That does not mean withdrawal from the world. We can be in the world, but not of it. Distractions are everywhere. Moderation is a very sensible thing. Is it a good individual choice, with good eternal consequences? The choice is up to us. We can get our reward now or get a reward later.

The other obvious question is, what are simple people? They are people who say what they mean, and mean what they say. They are not in deception. What they say, they feel in their heart. They can be led by the blind. The blind leading the blind—that is not a good thing. The more we are led by God, the less susceptible we are to being fooled. The truth is not falsified. There are many modern Pharisees and Scribes. False prophets abound. Though, there are many kind people. To be simple in heart is a good thing. They are sheep in sheep's clothing, not wolves. If you think about it, you will conclude luck is not real. Everything is meant to be. Like the Indian saying goes, "There are two wolves. One was mean, cruel, hateful, and vicious. The other wolf was kind, compassionate, loving, and caring. Which one wins? The one you feed." Tabor Hermon

Eleven hours in Morgue

A man was in very bad physical health—to the point of dying. He was in a hospital and died. They took him to the morgue. Eleven hours later, his family was called and told to get to the hospital. They thought this was very strange, as they did not know anyone in the hospital.

When they arrived, the man was alive and in good health. As amazing as this was, his mother never cried or went to the hospital. She knew all would be fine. *How? By believing what she could not see.*

Guardian Angel

A woman went to Niagara Falls. She lived in Baltimore. Her husband was overseas in the military. The return trip was unusual to say the least. She took a bus that had a stopover in NYC. It was 1:30 a.m. Her transfer was on the other end of the terminal. As she was walking along, an old lady started walking and talking with her. She was very friendly. About halfway, the young girl saw an elevator that went to her level. She decided to get on. The old lady tried to tell her not to do it. After getting on, two young men who had been following her got on. She knew she was in a bad place. The old lady said, "Come on, honey, let's walk." The two guys blocked her from exiting. At that point, the old lady motioned with her finger to come to her. The two guys fell down. She told the young girl to always be aware of her surroundings. After that, the old lady disappeared. Guardian angel?

Window Fall

This actually happened to my girlfriend. In keeping with my anonymous promise, I will not reveal her name. This miracle involves a woman who went to help her daughter. We are all born to help each other. The daughter had thyroid problems and lived 260 miles away. As the room upstairs was being cleaned, the window was raised. There was still a screen and curtain, but that was not enough. Apparently, the screen was easily removed. The two-year-old grandbaby fell out of the window on the second floor. It was about fourteen feet high. The woman tried to grab her, but it was too late. In a vision, she saw the child fall on a green canopy. My mom also had a dream about a child falling on a canvas that night. The child was taken to the hospital after the fall. The doctor said she was fine, and the girl was out playing the next day. The next day, the woman was talking to her daughter and said she was so glad that the canopy was there. Much to her surprise, her daughter informed her there was no canopy. That is a miracle!

Heart Light

I met a lady in a small restaurant she owned. Her story is truly amazing. It started as follows: My friend and I were comforting a dying friend. My other friend was in the hospital dying from pancreatic cancer. For those who do not know much about cancer, that is the worst illness. It has a very low survival rate. My friend and I were sitting there and praying for her. We were totally surprised by what happened next. As we were sitting there, a beautiful beam of light came into the room. It was a dark room. We could not make any sense of where it came from. The light was on the wall in the shape of a heart. As we looked at the heart, it began to pulsate. I was able to capture a picture on my phone. I was shaking so bad that you could not see the shape of the light. The beauty of that heart was a strength to me and my friend. My other friend was dying, but the grace was for us to be comforted by the Lord. When you get up in the morning and pray for spiritual eyes and ears, things happen. I truly believe that this was a divine miracle. Truly a blessing in my life.

Voice Inside

The following is from a person I met in an art museum. He is a curator. He was traveling down a two-lane highway in the country. He heard a voice inside say pull over. He had no idea what was going on. Anyway, he pulled over. About ten seconds later, a truck towing a wide mobile home went by the other way. Had he not listened, it probably would have been a life-ending accident. Listening meant the difference of living and dying.

Ashes

This is a personal miracle that happened to me, the author. My wife died from breast cancer. It spread to her lungs, bones, and brain. At the end, we communicated by blinks and hand clasps. She wanted to be cremated. We lived on a beautiful lake, and her favorite spot is where I decided to pour the ashes out of the urn. When I poured the ashes, they did not sink. Instead, they shot out about 150 feet. It was not a windy day. There is no logical explanation to what happened. I do not claim to know why this occurred. I just know what I saw had meaning.

JC Screwdriver

This happened a long time ago, about fifty years. It is still relevant today, maybe even more so. My mom worked with my dad in a business. One day when my dad was at the bank, a man came in. He had very bad intentions and asked my mom if she was alone. She said her husband would be right back. At that point, he grabbed a screwdriver. He started spinning it around. His next move was to stab my mom. She said to herself, *In the name of Jesus Christ, you will not harm me.* The man threw the screwdriver down and took off running. Nothing happened. There is power in that name.

Liver Tumor

This next miracle involves cancer. A man had a tumor in his liver. It was about the size of a golf ball. X-rays were done to show the tumor. After numerous trips to the oncologist (cancer doctor), there was a thirty-day break. During that time, the man envisioned the tumor going away. Another X-ray shocked the doctors. It revealed that the tumor was completely gone. The power of belief is strong. The tumor never returned. Hallelujah!

Pancreatic Cancer Prayer

This is a story of prayer. A man's mother was experiencing pain. She went to have it checked out and found she had pancreatic cancer. That is 95 percent fatal. After much crying, she turned to prayer. Many subsequent trips resulted in the same bad news. All her family and friends prayed. The doctors had decided on major surgery. One last X-ray was performed. The tumor was gone. The power of prayer is very real and very underestimated.

Rain Sleep

Many miracles happen on the road, as told in this harrowing experience. I was going about seventy miles per hour on a highway in the rain. It was mid afternoon, but I had eaten a big lunch. I was very sleepy and looking for a rest stop. After going about fifty miles, I fell asleep. The car went off the highway. It was the only place with no billboards on that stretch.

The bumpiness of the mud woke me up. I was about thirty feet off the road, heading straight toward a fence. While far from wide awake, I knew that there was something drastically wrong with that picture. I steered back to the road. There was no sliding, even none on the right lane of the highway. Considering the speed and rain, I found it hard to believe. God took the wheel. I could not have done that. I was very shaken up but totally fine. There is something left for me to do in this life. I thank God for my life.

Thirty Angels

A man had a heart attack; though he did not know it. He worked all day. On top of that, he was stabbed by his girlfriend too. Needless to say, he was in bad shape—very close to death. After going to the hospital that evening, he was told he was minutes away from dying.

The knife barely missed his heart. Inquiring about angels in the hospital, he was told there were about thirty reported each month. The chance of survival was very small. The knife wound disappeared. Guardian angels were at work, and the man made a full recovery.

Rising Roses

A lady went camping with her daughters. Inside the tent, they had red roses, which had wilted. To their astonishment, the roses sprang back up. They were almost dead! There is no earthly explanation for this occurrence. Seeing is believing.

Seatbelts Off

My brother-in-law and I were driving to see a couple of family members. It was late at night. I was driving his pickup, and an animal unexpectedly came onto the road. I slammed on my brakes, trying not to hit it. I swerved off the side of the road. Trying to get back on the road, I hit a pole. I went into a spin. Before that happened, neither I nor my brother-in-law had our seatbelts on. My brother-in-law was unconscious. We missed a bunch of cars that were very close. I was going about sixty-five miles per hour. I ended up on the median.

After the smoke and dust cleared, I went to get out of my vehicle. To my surprise, my seatbelt was on. I did not think anything of it at the time. I got out and looked around the truck. I woke my brother-in-law up. His seatbelt was on too. Later on that night, I got to thinking about it. I thought God must have really been watching us. I am sure I did not put my seatbelt on. It was a miracle. I am lucky to be alive.

Cancer Prayer

It was just another ordinary day. Working, eating, and sleeping. My dad was very stressed about something. So I said, "What's wrong?" He said, "Your mom is in a lot of pain. Her side is hurting." We took her to the hospital, and they took an X-ray. They spotted something on her pancreas. So we went to MD Anderson Cancer Center. We got it confirmed that it was pancreatic cancer. It was pretty hard to deal with. They said she only had three months to live. She just cried herself to sleep every night. We walked through it. The day came that she had to get surgery done on her pancreas and remove her spleen. They were going to remove her spleen and the tumor on her pancreas. We were all scared, all my relatives. It was a five-hour surgery.

The doctor came out very straight-faced. My thoughts were she had died. After that, he started smiling. He said, "Your mom is just fine. We think she will make it." We were all happy. About a month went by. On a checkup, the doctors said they spotted something on her lungs with an X-ray. It got us to thinking again. We thought she had more tumors. We got scared again. We were all holding hands. We all set down at the table and started saying prayers. The goal was to remove all the evil and badness. The doctors said it was a tumor, and they needed to do more tests. It was positive on the cancer. I called everyone I knew and asked all to pray. They did one more test. It had disappeared completely. There was nothing there, it was gone. That truly is a miracle.

Closet Pants

I was looking for a pair of pants that were on a hanger. It was very crowded in the closet, and I could not see or find my pants. The next thing I knew, the pants literally jumped in my hands.

I just thanked God.

Green Lights

I often get a green-light driving. Not always, but most of the time. Counting the lights, I realized twelve green lights in a row was more than a coincidence. There are no coincidences. I realized that does not make me better than anyone, just very thankful. I just smile and say, "Thank you, God."

Often, I expect a red light to turn green. Sometimes, it does not. Sometimes, I feel my patience is being tested.

Beach Disappearance

I walked the beach about fifteen miles a day. One day, a man approached me and started talking about God. He was with a large group of people playing volleyball. After talking for about five minutes, I walked up the beach for about fifteen minutes. I turned around to talk to the man, and he was gone. The whole group that played volleyball was gone. I never saw him again.

I'm not claiming he was an angel. I do not believe you can see angels with your physical eyes, only with spiritual eyes. I believe God puts us here to help one another, not ourselves.

Heart Artery

I was in Denver, Colorado. My dad got a call at about three o'clock in the morning. It was from his brother. He said, "Something is up with Dad. We do not know what it is yet. You have got to come down here." My grandfather was in Lubbock, Texas. My dad flew there. While my mom, my sisters, and I drove there in our vehicle. He was in the hospital. The doctors could not figure what was wrong with him. It was his heart. He had five open heart surgeries prior to this. We were there for about a week. The best doctors in the world were there—one from Germany, New York, and all kinds of different countries. They said they had never seen anything like this before. He had an artery grow off another artery and into his heart. The doctors said they did not know an artery could grow like tree branches. After about a week, they said there was really nothing they can do with him. They had never seen this before in their life. My grandmother looked at them. She said, "Do what you can. If you can't do anything at all, I understand." So they tried to think of an idea to get the artery out of his heart, without damaging the heart. He had about a fifteen percent chance of survival. It was about a twelve-hour surgery. They came out and said they still had not got it out. Another two hours went by, and they came back out. They said they had got it all. He was the only man in the world to have that happen. It was a miracle that he was alive. I am truly blessed to have him around.

Hip Surgery

It was a simple thing, but it hit me, when I needed to be hit. I had a hip replacement. It was the second time, and I was just going through the motions. I was only in my early forties, very young to have two hip replacements. While I was in the recovery bed, the stitches were very uncomfortable and extremely swollen. I am allergic to ibuprofen, so the doctors could not do anything about the swelling. It was near my buttocks, and I could not lay flat. I could not turn over. I simply could not get comfortable. So I had nothing but my Bible. I had no visitors, and nobody came to see me. I went into my Bible and started reading. I was suffering, but I was suffering for the cause. I was not suffering emotionally. Because it was a physical ailment, I was in pain. I was still very much in joy. At one point, I could not get any sleep. I was getting very frustrated. I was physically and emotionally frustrated. I barely got the prayer out when something amazing happened. I had made up my mind, I was going to pray about the inflammation in the incision area. I felt a tremendous decrease instantly. I felt like someone had let air out of a balloon. I felt the stitch area, and the stitches were gone. It felt as smooth as a baby's bottom. Praise God!

Aloe Vera Cancer

This is a story about a guy I worked with. His wife had stage 4 cancer. Someone had told her about a new product that comes from the aloe vera plant. It had shown promise as a cancer fighter. His wife started taking it, and now she no longer has cancer.

South Padre Bridge

I was recently at South Padre Island, Texas. The bridge had recently been out. A tugboat had hit the middle. It caused a section of the bridge to fall. It occurred at about 2:00 a.m. Nobody knew it was out for about one hour. People would drive on the bridge and fall into the ocean. A guy that went in the ocean said his car was sinking. He could not get out. He said his mother had passed away a few months before, and he swears that his mother pulled him out of the car. She then took him to the top of the water, and he lived!

Leukemia

When my daughter was around twenty-three years old, she was diagnosed with leukemia. All the churches we knew in North Carolina and Houston, Austin, and Dallas, Texas all prayed. We asked our Lord Jesus to heal her. She had her bone marrow checked. This was to determine which chemotherapy she would need. When the results of the bone marrow came back, they said they had misdiagnosed. She did not have cancer. The original blood work said she definitely had leukemia. We all know it was our Lord Jesus Christ. Now, it has been seven years. Her blood platelets got real high. She needed an extremely low dose of chemotherapy. The oncologist told her not to get pregnant. Well, she got pregnant. He told her she needs to abort because the baby would have many defects. He told her, she might bleed to death. She said, "No, God gave me this baby. I am going to have it." For nine months, her blood platelets were completely normal. She did not need any medication. An ultrasound showed no abnormalities. And my grandbaby was born normal. God's grace and mercy were evident.

Angel Visit

On our way to work at a Christian school, a car pulled out in front of us, and there was no time to stop, so we broadsided the vehicle. One child knocked off the mirror in the front seat from the back, and the others were shaken but okay.

We were waiting to get information exchanged when a man from literally nowhere came up and asked if there was anything he could do. I said my son needed some ice to put on his forehead. Seconds later, he brought it and disappeared. To this day, my son has a scar reminding us that he was visited by an angel from heaven above.

To God be the glory!

Multi-Myeloma

My wife was healed five years ago of multi-myeloma. Her spine broke from tumors deposited by the cancer. Today she is cancer-free.

Radio

I was working on a recreational vehicle. Replacing a fuse, I turned all the electrical breakers off in the trailer. The radio kept playing, even though everything else stopped. I thought, *That is strange.* So I went outside to unplug the power. The radio kept playing. There were no batteries.

Rain Drought

This is a story about rain. I believe it was 2009. There had been a drought for about eight months. I told a friend that it was going to rain. He was skeptical to say the least. It had not rained in eight months. His words were, "It will not rain a drop." About one minute later, it was raining hard.

A few days later, a lady said, "I sure hope it rains more."

I responded, "I know it is going to rain." It rained again.

Her husband came up to me, and said, "I heard you make it rain."

I laughed and said, "God makes it rain." A couple days later, it rained again. This time, it only rained where I was. I got in my car, only to see it was not raining elsewhere. That week, I called seven churches and visited seven churches. I simply said, "Let us all pray for rain this week." I received answers of "It will not hurt. We too have already prayed." All eventually agreed to pray for rain. That week, it poured. I thought, *Where is your faith?* Never saw any of them again. Did not need to!

Paramedic

One day when I was going out to the mailbox, I tripped and fell down. When I looked up, a man across the street had a package of envelopes in his hand. He said, "Lady, don't move. I am a paramedic." He helped me up. I dusted myself off. I turned around to thank him, and he was gone. I could not see him anywhere. I was so astonished.

Job Voice

It was early morning. I had a job interview at 8:30 a.m. I was actually studying the interview questions till 2:30 the night before. Anyway, I was sleeping. My alarm had gotten disabled from a power outage. All of a sudden, I heard a voice at 7:00 a.m. It said, "Time to get up, buddy. Let's go." I jerked myself awake. I showered, shaved, and got ready. I was on time for the interview and got the job. It was all because a little voice in my head. It told me to get up and move.

OKC Wreck

When I was a kid, I had a miracle. I was running across the freeway in Oklahoma City. I got hit by a car. I had two friends with me. The first was in front of me. They were not hit. An old man hit me, and I went up into his windshield. I was in such shock, I did not know I was hurt. I was lying on the ground. It is a miracle that I am still alive. I thank God for it. That is my earliest miracle.

Run Over Twice

I got run over twice in the same day. The first time was around three o'clock in the morning. I was leaving work at Whataburger. A drunk driver hit me. The same night, I was hit by an eighty-three-year-old man. He was on his way home and had a heart attack. He died in his car.

He was doing about seventy-six miles per hour when he hit me. The doctors said I would never walk again. I have a titanium kneecap, and my back is broken all the way down.

I got up and walked away from the scene of the accident. God kept me walking, talking, and moving. After this happened, my wife left me. The reason was that I will not stop doing the things of God, and it made me sad.

I have no home, family, that I know of. God provides for me every single day. I live by faith and prayer. I have never been let down. Even when the devil tried to stop me, God still provided. People looked at me and automatically think I am a bum. I am not a bum. I get out and work. I make CDs. I sell them on the street. I believe God will never leave me or forsake me. We are to go out to the highways and byways. If we are his sheep, we will share the word with all. If a person is spiritually hungry, we are supposed to feed them. We are to teach truth. People get caught up in good and evil. We are supposed to take the good and the bad, as water off a duck's back. I thank God for everything. Whether good or bad, it is all shaping us. It is all part of his plan to make us into who he wants us to be.

I do not claim to know everything. I do not want to know everything. Every person on this earth is perfect in God's eyes. I do not know where my next meal will come from. God knows. My next bed could be the sidewalk.

Houston Red Truck

We were in Houston at a gas station. My truck kept cutting off. I got it started but had to drive with both hands. I had to keep it revved up. I was using the gas pedal and brake at the same time. I could not stop long. I was trying to get out of the station. The traffic was very heavy, and I could not move. Out of nowhere, a big red tractor trailer blocked the traffic. I was able to get out. As soon as I turned out, I looked in my rearview mirror. The truck was gone. I looked all around me. It was nowhere to be found. I know a truck that big can't move fast. This all happened in less than five seconds.

Boxer

When I was born, I came out upside down. The umbilical cord was wrapped around my neck. I died shortly after birth. Ten minutes later, I was revived on a respirator. Normally, a person has many problems of breathing after that. I have no problems breathing.

I am a boxer. Born fighting and still fighting.

Purple Heart

We were walking into a parallel area in Vietnam. It is called Bolloey Woods. I got my first chance to see the communist. My first lieutenant saw a foxhole. He jumped in, only to find it was an R&R station for the communist.

He said, Okay, guys, let's go get them." That was a major mistake. All I carried was my radio and an M-16 gun.

I didn't even put on my shirt. I thought it would be very short. Next thing I know, I see four enemies.

I looked down at my arm; it was spinning like a clock.

I lost my weapon. I heard a thump behind me. I said to myself, *One of us is going to die.* A medic arrived on the scene. I rolled over on him, and I took a blast in my back. Apparently the morphine had taken effect. I had radio contact. I was told, "We are going to get you out."

I said, "No, I have got to tell you where these people are." I spent the next two hours telling the battalion chief where we were. It was with a few cuss words in there, and I am sorry. I received a purple heart and a silver star for this. I figured I would die anyway. The good Lord was on my side. When I rolled over, I thought I was done. I then heard the words, "It is not your time." It was like someone was next to me talking. I told the battalion commander where the foxholes and bunkers were.

White Bird

A long time ago, when I was sixteen years old, I had an incredible experience. It was around 10:30. I looked in the sky and saw a huge white bird. It was bigger than an airplane, with a lot of light in it. It was moving in slow motion. It was the most beautiful thing I had ever seen. It is hard to comprehend all that, but it was true. Not only did I see it, my sister and brother saw it. It was like the Holy Spirit. It had everlasting life. We called in to see if others had seen it. No other person saw it. It was just meant for us. My brother had just gotten out of prison, and that was a good sign. It was unbelievable. I will never forget it.

Lymphoma

I was diagnosed with B cell lymphoma when I was fifteen. I was actually misdiagnosed for about a year. I had a tumor in my leg. I noticed it was growing very large. It was actually growing inside my body. That summer, I was diagnosed with cancer. They said it had gotten so bad that I had to do very intense chemotherapy. This lasted two months, with a break for my body to recover. I got very sick. The strange thing about it was for whatever reason, I knew I was not going to die. I was not scared. I believe God told me that I would survive. Fortunately, by the grace of God, I did survive. I am now twenty-five years old.

Job

I was directed by God, I think. I took a job that I did not think I could do. I had not been trained for this job. I followed his guidance with good faith. I ended up doing the job for ten years, very successfully.

Head on Wreck

I was involved in a car accident. I was in my brother's vehicle in 1995. The driver coming toward us fell asleep. His vehicle hit us head on. My brother was killed, and the three people in the other vehicle were also killed. Somehow, I lived through that accident. It was a high-speed collision over seventy miles per hour.

The miracle that came after that is my wife and I had four children. We had no children at that time. My oldest son is a teenager, and we had three daughters after that. I guess the miracle of that is the generations that ensued. Also, the lives that will be passed on. I miss my brother and feel horrible for the three people in the other vehicle. God saw me through that difficult time. I received the strength to carry on. That is all a miracle.

Dead Brother

I saw a truck coming toward us. So I moved my vehicle over to the side of the road. I was on the paved shoulder. My brother was on the passenger's side. He yelled, "Oh!" The truck hit us head-on. It was so hard that it knocked us backward. The passenger side was on the bottom. The driver side was on the top. I felt like I was almost knocked out. I just prayed to the Lord to just take us home. My nose was broken. I had to have a plate in my hand. Then someone came to the door, not too long after the accident. My right foot was broken, and the door would not open. The really sad part was I had to step on my dead brother's body to get out. The ambulance came after about a half hour. I was then taken to the hospital. After numerous surgeries, I was able to walk. God blessed me with the ability to have a healthy life after that. I ask the question, "Why did I survive?"

You think you know why; then, you are not so sure.

Intestine Outside

My granddaughter was born with her intestines on the outside. There was no pediatric clinic in town. They were not equipped for this. The doctors kept her there for three days. They thought she was going to die. They finally sent her to the children's hospital in San Antonio. She was in an ICU for twenty-eight days. They decided to wait till she got older before they did surgery on her. A lot of prayers were prayed for her to live. On a Friday, the doctor said if her bowels did not move by Monday, she would die. There was a lot of prayer that weekend. On Sunday, her bowels moved. The doctor that delivered her had never seen this. There was a Christian surgeon that happened to be in the hospital. He came in and asked, "What are you guys going to do?" They really did not know what to do. He prayed about it. He put her intestines back in and sowed her up. That happened before she was sent to San Antonio.

She also had a tumor about the size of an orange. They decided to wait till she was one to remove it. To their shock, it was about the size of a nickel. She now has two children in her twenties. She has not had any problems. She is very blessed with good health. She is a Christian woman. She is raising her kids in the Christian faith.

Brain

A boy was born without the use of all his brain. The doctors did not expect him to make it. They gave him little to no chance. The doctors were totally wrong.

He not only survived but is a very intelligent sixteen-year-old today. He does have coordination problems. When he gets tired, he wobbles a little bit. Mentally, he is fine. There was much prayer for him. God is with those who believe in him.

C-Section

My daughter was born a couple of weeks early. We were watching the Baltimore Colts game with a bunch of friends. I knew something did not feel right. After rushing to the hospital, my daughter was not breathing right. Also, her heart was not beating right. They did an emergency C-section. It was weird to think something was wrong. That was our miracle.

Prison Overcomer

A man was in prison ten years for drugs. He had no direction or hope. After his release, he got a master's degree and a good job. He also got married and had two kids. Now very happy, he attributes everything to God. There is always hope!

Wreck Scratches

I was driving back to Virginia after my father passed away. I was very tired and sick. I was going about seventy-five or eighty miles per hour. I fell asleep at the wheel. I woke up after hitting an eighteen-wheeler truck. My car was about ten feet in the air. I crash-landed and slid to the left of the highway. When I got out of the car, all I had was minor cuts on my hand. That was from the broken glass. I looked on the side of the road. There was a sixty-foot ravine on the right. It would have surely killed me.

Five-Story Fall

The following miracle is from a Turkish Muslim. Turkish people believe in peace to a degree that is major. They will not even kill an ant. The custom of eating on the ground has some merit to it—you get full much quicker.

Every creature is part of life. A child fell five stories high, and he landed on a car top. He only sustained minor injuries. That is fifty feet!

Starting Over

I had a car accident around 2001. I was ejected from the vehicle. I landed after 189 feet. I suffered facial injuries, head lacerations, and head trauma. I broke my arm in four places. I also dislocated my shoulder. My right ear was torn off. I had five fingers torn off. Miraculously they were put back on at the hospital. Thankfully, there was a meeting of neurologist from around the world. Some of the best trauma doctors were there. I went through five and a half months of rehabilitation. I had to learn to walk and talk again.

I worked on my gait. Every detail was attended to. The Lord gave me life not once, but twice. Jesus saves through prayer. I am now walking normally.

God's Work

Basically, the most miraculous thing to happen is the revelation of God's work in me. The fact of the matter is people get complacent about mainstream religion. Unfortunately, that is contrary to understanding the truth of God. Being in the mainstream is what got us into trouble in the past. We tend to go with the mainstream. It will get us into trouble again. People tend to believe the so-called norm is fine. Again and again the past has proven not to support this line of thought. People tend to do what is wrong and call it right. People look for God outside of our temple, which is our body. They do not realize that the Lord said, "There will be many coming in my name." To me, that is all the churches. The kingdom of heaven is within you. People rely on the outside, not the inside. It is not what goes inside your body that is bad; it is what comes out. That has revolutionized the way I think.

New Life-Job

M iracles happened in my life; this is actually how I came to Christ. God brought me to my knees. I was in the military, and my life was pretty set. I had a girlfriend. The miracle involved my girlfriend cheating on me and the consequent breakup. Also, I was losing my job in the military. Medically, I could no longer do my job. The miracle came through harsh circumstances. I cried out to God for help. I had a life, not knowing Christ. It was not a miracle, as people think of today. God brought me through with his love, and I am fine now.

Devil Driving

I experienced a miracle where God spared my life. One day I was traveling. I had been traveling all night. I became very sleepy. I remember opening my eyes. And I could see the clouds in front of me as I was traveling. Suddenly, they began to take the form of a face. That face drifted from the sky down to the highway in front of me. It started laughing at me. I went through the mouth of this figure. It scared me so bad, I woke up. It dawned on me what this figure was in the shape of.

It was the devil. He was laughing at me for being so stubborn. I kept driving when I was so sleepy. But God brought me out of that. Believe me, it was such a terrifying experience that I was wide awake. It saved me from falling asleep at the wheel, all through the grace of God.

Birth

My mom did not know she was pregnant. And she was in love with my dad. She had a miscarriage and tried to kill herself, but she did not know there was another baby in there. I am now a teenager. I was the other baby. It is a miracle that I was born.

$20

A lady was working. Then a person she did not even know gave her twenty dollars. She said, "God said to do this." The interesting part of this is she said it was not from herself.

Miracle Child

My mother had a cyst on her ovary. It ruptured in New Orleans. They cut her open and saw me. The doctors said, "Not yet." They sewed her back up. She did not know she was pregnant. I believe I was a miracle child.

Guesthouse

I graduated college over the summer. Our house was by the Frio River. I moved there and worked at a family friend T-shirt shop. While I went shopping with my grandmother, I got hired on the spot. It was pretty far though. It was a town that I loved. Then reality hit. I did not know where I was going to live.

I said, "I would try out the job." My first day at work, an old lady came in. She wanted to know my story.

She said, "You cannot be driving from your river house. It is too far, and there is fog. We have a guesthouse down the road, if you would live there." I had just met this lady. We went to dinner and talked about it. Her husband had been a veterinarian for fifty years. He and my papa worked cattle sales together forty years ago. So they knew each other. I ended up living in the guesthouse for about two months. I eventually found my own place. That is kind of my own little miracle.

Hard Work

I am a twenty-year-old male. I started working when I was sixteen at a restaurant. I had saved money throughout my life. I had money, even at that young age. I started working for an energy company with my brother. Although it was lucrative, I was unable to get around. I was young and had no car or license. When I turned seventeen, I made the decision to join the military. I went into the recruiter's office. I signed up to be in the marine corps. I graduated high school and joined the marines. It was a life-transforming experience. At the age of nineteen, I had saved $30,000. I had a hard work ethic, and I was a very strong believer. My military experience taught me how to be around other people. I had previously stayed away from other people. I used to be a very shallow introvert and prejudge people, and I was not really interested in getting to know others outside of my comfort zone.

The military taught me many life lessons. For example, you must rely on others to make it. I realized everybody is the same. I am now twenty years old and have a business partner who is nineteen. I am blessed to be with him. When I met him, he did not meet the qualifications I was looking for. Because of my mind-set of everybody is a friend, I was able to get closer. Eventually, we both had like minds and were ambitious. Initially, we brainstormed for hours on different ways to make money. We decided we were going to open a yogurt business. We figured people would become conscious of their health. We established our own franchise and were very successful. Through a stroke of luck, we found something better. My brother was a country singer. We went out of town to watch him. We were dressed very nice, and we went to a very nice mall. We did not expect anything walking around. We had some successful gentleman approach us, and they asked what we had going. They were looking for sharp, young people to expand their market. We told them we were very busy, but we exchanged numbers. Long story short, we made a lot of money with these guys. Hard work and perseverance does pay off.

Pilot Eject

A pilot went through a terrible crash. He had to have his spleen removed. He lived his life as normal as possible. He had gotten a pilot's license after the military. He experienced aircraft failure in enemy territory. He was in very high altitude when he ejected. It would normally kill a person, but he is alive and fine without his spleen.

License

A girl was looking for her license while cleaning her car. Even though she searched very intently, she could not find it. She was subsequently pulled over by a police officer. She looked where she had cleaned before. Her license was there, and nothing happened. She was certain it was not there during the cleaning.

Car Stopping

I was driving on a future highway. The only highway part completed was about 10 miles. I had my car for about one year before this. I never had any problems with it. The brakes went out on me. I was speeding about 85 or 90. I was in a rush. Traffic was at a dead stop. I put the pedal all the way to the floor to no avail. There were about 50 cars in the traffic. Without explanation, the car cut off by itself, and stopped. My life flashed before my eyes. I remember it well to this day.

Automatic Writing

I was sitting in mechanical engineering class. As a near 40 non traditional student. What happened was a study question came out of my mind. I did not even contemplate. It was down on paper without my knowing. Immediately, I went to the local church and prayed. I thanked God. I knew at that instant, that I was going to graduate.

Nonbeliever

A man cleaning tables had serious problems with his knee. There were tumors in there, and the veins did not go into it right. If it blew, he would die. A coworker prayed over him. He was not completely healed but enough to cause complete disbelief. The very next day, he was so much better. This is a story of the power that is out there. This man was a nonbeliever. Now he has his own Bible and totally believes.

Tumor Gone

About ten years ago, my mother was diagnosed with cancer. They found a tumor in her ovaries. It was the size of a grapefruit. The biopsy led doctors to a firm removal conclusion. In the meantime, my family started praying. They were already heavily into prayer. The doctors did one last ultrasound. There was nothing there. The tumor was completely gone.

Eighty-One-Year-Old Heart

I am eighty-one years old. In my life, the Lord has pulled me out of three situations of death. The first that I recall, I was home in the morning. I started feeling dizzy and nauseated, and there were pains in the middle of my chest.

I was having a heart attack. At that time, I was working for an insurance company. I knew all the symptoms. I told my wife to call an ambulance, because I was having a heart attack. The doctor at the hospital said I had not had a heart attack, but I was about to have one. I took something to unclog the heart arteries. It did not work. They did an angioplasty operation. It basically was throwing in a device to open one of my heart valves. It was literally a blown-up balloon to expand the arteries. I was in the hospital for eight days.

One time, I went to buy a guitar, and a young teenager ran over me outside. It was on Father's Day. A helicopter came, and I was told I might die from my injuries. Thank God, I am fine today. God always comes through for me. That is why I am a true believer and Christian. The Lord makes miracles. The Bible says you will have life everlasting, and I really do.

Brain Swelling

This is regarding my daughter. She was about thirteen years old when she was involved in an accident. At that time, we lived in a suburban area of a large city. She and a friend decided to go bike-riding. There was a lot of industry around that area. My daughter was riding her bike, and then the brakes quit working. She was hit by a vehicle coming out of one of the industry areas. She landed on the curb of the road. Very quickly, her friend came to the house. She told me my daughter had been in an accident. Upon arriving, I saw that it was obvious that she was in shock. She kept calling my name. I whispered in her ear, "Remember God is always with you." I will never forget that. We started praying together, and she finally calmed down. The ambulance came by, picked her up, and took her to the hospital. The doctor told us her brain was swelling. After taking X-rays, they realized she hit herself on the brainstem. They said there would be a lot of complications in the future. She would be having seizures and would not be the same person as she was in the past. She stayed in the hospital about two weeks.

The doctors were amazed. Once she got home, she was wobbly and uncoordinated. This lasted about one week. After that, she started getting back on her feet. She never took a lot of medication. We have a lot of faith, and we prayed about it a lot. We feel God cured her. She is now thirty-two and fine. She is doing great. I feel this was a miracle.

Field Disappearance

This happened about a month ago while I was walking. I had moved into a friend's sister's house. I was walking to the coffee shop. Then I saw a guy and a lady walking past a surplus store. I did not think anything about it at first.

Then I noticed they seemed like mystical figures. I do not know why, it was a feeling I had. I looked back toward them, and they were gone. There was not any place to go to. They were in a field, and I looked back in five seconds.

Wheels on Plane

There was a jet airplane about to make a routine landing. However, the wheels would not come down. After trying repeatedly, the pilot made a decision to crash land. After a period of time, the jet was about to land on the belly. On the final approach, something miraculous happened. The wheels came down ten seconds before landing. The plane made a safe landing.

Seventeen-Year-Old

When my mom was pregnant with me, she was in a terrible accident. This happened in 1996. It was in a minivan. There were seven people in the car, and my mom and aunt were both pregnant. There was a big collision. The van rolled five times. My mom had her seatbelt on, but my aunt did not. My aunt lost her baby. I wanted to come out of the womb, but I was born two months later. It is a miracle that I am alive. I am a now seventeen years old and healthy.

Railroad Track

A man was crossing a railroad track. He had a very strange feeling. After he crossed, he looked behind him. A man with his three young kids stopped on the track.

It was a suicide. The train hit the van. The man was killed instantly. The man was getting a divorce with his wife. It was a "I cannot have the kids, you cannot have them" situation. The three kids survived. The man with the strange feeling helped the kids out of the van. This possibly saved their lives. They are fine today. A strong feeling came over the man, that something was about to happen. He saw the incident in his rearview mirror. This was ridiculous petty jealousy. At first, the man would not talk about this event. As time went by, he began to feel good about his role in the wreck.

Pocano Cliff

My dad grew up in Pennsylvania. It was in the Pocano mountains. It snows there, and the roads get pretty icy. As a kid, he went to church quite a bit. One day he was driving up the mountain. He lost control of his vehicle, and there are no guardrails, just some poles and chain links. They were spinning out of control. They were heading to the end of the road. My friend's dad looked at my dad and asked what was going to happen. All my dad could say is, "I am sorry." They stopped right before going down a cliff. Their momentum seemed to stop.

Four-Year-Old Spleen

When I was four, I was in a bad car wreck. I had internal bleeding and a ruptured spleen. The Lord gave me two spleens. After removing the spleen, I was fine. Apparently, God knew I would need an extra spleen. That was pretty miraculous.

Five ODS

When I was in my twenties, I had five drug overdoses on heroin. Five is not a coincidence; it is the number of grace. The last time I overdosed, I was pronounced clinically dead for ten minutes at the Grace Lutheran hospital. I was not saved. I believed in God and thought I was a Christian. I was a heathen. I know that God saved my life on that occasion and many other times. God knew that in the future, I would preach his word, would testify for him, and give him glory. I believe the reason that I lived and a lot of my friends died is because God knew they would never say yes. He left them to a reprobate mind, as the Bible says. What happens, happens. But I was protected by his angels. Just like Job, you can attack him, but you cannot have his soul. God allowed the devil to attack me and deceive me into doing the things I did. Because God knew I would one day say yes, I was protected. That is just one of the things God did for me. That was thirty years ago.

Brain Bleed

In 2002, I was bleeding in my brain for about eight months. Every time I went to the doctor, he said it was sinus problems. This happened repeatedly. Finally, in May of that year, I got severely sick at work. I am a schoolteacher. When I went for a checkup that Saturday, the doctor said I was bleeding on my brain. I was put in the emergency ward. I had a large blood clot on the back of my head. Also, he had gathered my family. He said I would not make it through the night. It would be a miracle if I did, because of where the bleeding was. Then they asked me many questions. They did not want to get involved because they thought someone did that to me. Thank God my sister worked there. She went to the head of the hospital. They were told to begin treating me. Also, the Lord had a neurologist there. He knew exactly what was going on with me. He said I had a very rare sinus condition. It was called sinus thrombosis. It caused the brain to bleed from blisters bursting. That happened eleven years ago. The Lord did spare my life.

I give this testimony that he is a wonderful God. He will heal you, if you trust and believe in him.

As I said earlier, the doctor said there was no way I could live. The doctors just sent me home to die. They said there was nothing they could do. With prayer and hope, I was going to a miracle service at church. I lifted my hands to praise God. I felt tingling all over my head. When I went back to the doctor, all the blood clots were gone. I give all glory to God.

Skateboard

I had a skateboard, and I had a bad accident with it. I hurt my back very bad. I then went to a Bible study, and they prayed over me. During that time, I felt like something touched me. After that, it was amazing. I could breathe fine. The pain was gone!

Oklahoma Pictures

My sister moved to Oklahoma with my mom. My grandparents had both passed away. They had twenty-two kids. My sister was driving early in the morning to work. The windows were rolled down halfway to get that fresh air.

My mom's house was hit by a tornado. The house shifted off the concrete blocks by about a foot. One window broke. All the pictures fell down. The only pictures that were not affected were my grandmother's pictures and the Virgin Mary.

December 13 Drunk Driver

It was December 13, and I was coming home from a basketball game. The last thing I remember was sitting at a red light turning green. Then a drunk driver hit the back left side of my car. The car flipped over three times. I was in surgery for the next two hours. I woke up with no memory for two or three days. At that point, I was surprised to be alive. Everything came back, and my memory was totally restored.

Thyroid Cancer

I was having some thyroid issues. I went in for surgery to have half of it removed. They found out it was malignant. It was thyroid cancer, stage 3. I refused treatment. I prayed and believed. God healed me. That was two years ago. There has been no evidence of cancer in my body today. So praise God.

2:00 A.M. Wake Up

A lady at my church was telling a story. She was asleep in bed when she heard the baby monitor. The baby was at the other end of the house. Nothing happened. She woke up in the middle of the night at about 2:00 a.m. She was scared, but did not know why. She realized she had turned the baby monitor off. She went to check on her six-month-old son. When she arrived, he was convulsing. I believe it was an epilepsy attack. She helped him and probably saved his life. He is now thirteen years old. It was a miracle she woke at that time.

Soccer Pain

A man played soccer for many years. He then had a groin injury and went and had a CAT scan and MRI. The doctors said he was fine. That being said, he was still in a lot of pain. This lasted a couple weeks after the hospital visit. He then went to church and prayed for the pain to subside. The pain totally went away. He was pain-free.

Festival Wreck

I was downtown at a festival. I was having a lot of drinks. I am not old enough to drink, but I was very drunk. I do not remember walking to my car or getting in. I made it halfway home and fell asleep at the wheel. The whole car went over the guardrail. It popped all my tires, and the car was totaled, but I was not hurt at all. I was fine.

Black Cat

This was the time when I was with my ex-girlfriend. We had a black cat at home. We were going to sleep one night and saw two black cats at the foot of the bed. I grabbed one of the black cats. The other disappeared before our eyes. We both freaked out. We did not understand what had just happened. About three days later, my girlfriend talked about that night. She said when I grabbed the cat, my face lit up with light. She didn't want to tell me. She thought I would get mad. I thought that was pretty intriguing. I did see a light in the room. I thought it was car headlights shining in the room. She said, "No, it was actually coming out of your face."

Car Repair

My dad was very low on money. His car broke down on our street. He was trying to figure out the problem. He did not know much about cars, so he was heartbroken. He went inside the house, very dejected. He had little money and needed to get to work. He started praying. He went out to the car and looked under the hood. He pulled a part off the engine. He went to the auto supply and said he needed that part. It cost him $10. He put it on, and the car started right up. What makes this story amazing is he knew nothing about cars.

Kneecaps

I have had my kneecaps rebuilt since I got stabbed three times. I got shot in my kneecaps and hit over the head with a baseball bat. That all happened in less than three days. I guess I am stubborn—a walking miracle.

Indian Stalker

I was living in New York as a starving actress. I was going down the wrong path. I was partying every day. I was young.

One day, I got out of a theater. I was going home on the subway. Then I felt a person look at me. He was a man who looked kind of Indian. He looked at me with an intense look, not like "I think you are pretty" but a scary look. It was very intense. People around me were uneasy about his look. I was literally scared for my life. I was thinking, *Oh my God, if this man does not stop looking at me, I don't know what to do.* I thought I would get off on the next exit. Well, when the next stop came, he was just sitting there. I went to the exit, and he stayed there for a moment. I was relieved. Then I was horrified to see him jump up and follow me. I did not know what to do. I was in New York by myself and did not know anybody. A man saw him following me. He said, "Be careful, someone is following you."

I said, "I know. I am so scared, and I do not know what to do." I went into a twenty-four hour cafe/store. I was totally freaked out. I stayed for a while. Then the same man that said "Be careful" came in. He asked if I was okay. He gave me money to get a cab. I was so thankful, but I did not even know who he was. He put me in the cab. He then said, "Take care of yourself, Ruby." I asked him what his name was. He said his name was Jesus (Spanish). He was a Latino guy. I saw the guy following me. He watched the cab drive away. I felt he was going to kill me. The next day, I told some people that story. They asked, "How did he know your name?" I recalled that I never told him my name. What a coincidence that his name was Jesus.

Car Squeeze

A car in front of me came to a dead stop, and I stopped behind the car. There was a SIMI behind me. I was scared for my life as he was going fast. I went into the other lane. It was a narrow miss. I would have certainly been squeezed to death.

Eighteen-Wheeler

An eighteen-wheeler crashed into me from behind. My brother fell out of the vehicle. I was shocked to see that he just had scratches and bruises.

$10 Part

My husband had a pickup truck. It had quit working. He was a mechanic, so he worked and slaved yet was unable to get it to work. He prayed and he prayed and he prayed. He replaced every part he could think of. He spent every afternoon working on it. He could not get it to run. One day he was on his way to work in the rain and lightning. There was a man on the side of the road. He had a hood on. It was kind of like a raincoat. My husband very rarely picked up hitchhikers. For some reason this day, he did. He was a soft-hearted person. He pulled over and opened the passenger door. The man got in. My husband asked where he was going. He did not say anything, just motioned up the road. My husband tried to make small talk with him. He told about his truck having a lot of problems. He just kept talking about all the problems and working on the truck.

The man asked if he had tried such and such. My husband said, no, that never came to his mind. He did not think that was the problem. My husband got to the turnoff for work. He told the man, "This is where I need to let you off." He pulled off the road. The man got out, without ever showing his face. He did not say a lot, other than what he thought might be wrong with the truck. The man said thank you and disappeared. There was nowhere to remove himself on the road. He did not jump in the back of the car. No one else picked him up. My husband had an eerie feeling. He said he thought it was Jesus. He was very soft spoken.

My husband went to work. That evening, he decided to try what the man recommended. Then the truck started up. It was exactly what he was told by this person. He said, "There was no way this person could have gotten out of my sight." He maintained that he believes he picked up Jesus that day.

Prostate Cancer

A strange thing happened before my prostate operation in 2005. The night before my operation, I dreamed I saw myself walking down the hospital corridor. I was pushing the IV that was attached to my arm. Right at that moment, I knew the operation that I was going to have the next day would be successful. The good Lord was sending me a message that I was going to be okay.

I have been cancer-free for the last eight years.

Twenty-Five Beats a Minute

After my husband and I split up, I had to go to the hospital. My heartbeat had dropped to twenty-five beats a minute. They could not get my heart rate up. They had the alarms going off. They used every tool at their disposal. They called all my kids and my mom. They told my mom to say good-bye to me. All of a sudden, the lights went down low. There was a bright light. I came back through it after three and a half hours. I got to see all of my children flash in front of me. I do not know if God was telling me you have these three to live for. I came back through.

Stage 4 B Cancer

I was diagnosed with cancer four years ago. It was February 15. I had my surgery on March 25. It was a very aggressive type. I had stage 4 B cancer. I went through chemotherapy and radiation. I am still here. God gave me a second chance. I see the world different. I appreciate every day. The gift he gives me.

Camry

I was driving in the rain. I had a two-door Camry coupe. I was going down a hill. I saw a deer run out in front of me. I slowed down without an incident. I saw it pass. I naturally thought it was clear to go. Of course they always come in twos. The last one came at the last second. I had no time to react. I pulled my emergency brake and cut the wheel. Because it was slick, I started spinning. I was still in forward, but my car was sliding backward. The next thing I knew was I was watching the hill going down backward. I released the emergency brake. I also turned the wheel back. I ended up doing a 180-degree turn and was perfectly straight going down the hill. I was shaken up. However, I was completely fine. My arms and my heart were shaking. I could not keep the wheel straight. It was a crazy thing.

Hog Farm

In 1978, I was working on a farm in Indiana. It was in the cold winter. I was working with the hogs. I had never worked on a farm before. I stepped over a big grain auger and did not make it. It caught me in it. I was in the barn by myself. A lot of machinery was running. It was probably the most scared I had been in my life. I screamed. I thought my leg was going to be pulled off. I could actually feel the machine pulling me in it. I cried out to the other workers and said, "Oh, God, get me out of here." My boot literally was pulled off my foot. It was torn up by the machine. I usually wear tight leather boots. On that morning, I wore loose boots. I did not know why I wore those boots that day.

I wore loose rubber boots. If I had worn my other boots, I would have lost a foot, maybe a leg. I probably would have bled to death. I crawled out to the snow. The contrast of my blood was stark. My boss saw me from up a hill. He ran down, and I grabbed him. I went to a hospital. I told all the doctors and nurses that God kept my foot intact. They thought I was delirious. My friend from the farm said he had seen a mangled foot. He said that what he saw at the hospital was not the same foot. It was not mangled. I still have the scar and still have pain to this day. It hurts several times a day. That pain is a reminder that God kept my foot on. When I get tired walking, I think about I could be dead or not have a leg to walk on. That was a significant thing God did for me. Two weeks before, a guy had both arms cut off in that machine. If that boot did not come off, my foot would have been ground up. That is my miracle.

Stage 5 Cancer

My mother had cancer for twelve years. She had gone through everything. She was a guinea pig. She started with stage 5 cancer. The fact she is still alive is a miracle to me.

Eyeballs Out of Socket

This story is about a young man in the military. He was in the navy. He was a medic in the war in Iraq. At that time, he did not have any faith in God. Actually, he did not care about God. He was sent into battle. Then a very good friend of his was injured by a mine. His friend died, in spite of his effort to save him. It resulted in his eyes popping out and total blindness. He was in the hospital for eight months. Both eyes had bandages over them. The doctor told him he would never see again. At that point, he talked to God, even though he did not believe in God. He said to God, "If you really do exist, give me my sight back." He was very angry. His eyeballs were hanging out of his sockets. He had surgery with a blindfold put on afterward. The nurses checked on him periodically.

One day, he felt it was time to take the bandages off. But it was not the time to do this yet. It was something he felt like he needed to do. When he did, he started seeing light silhouettes. He started to recognize people walking by. The nurse that had taken care of him came in the room. She was shocked. He decided to get up and walk. Normally, they led him by the arm. This time, he led the nurse. He walked through the hall. Everybody was amazed. The doctor came and checked on him. He told him, "This must be a miracle. There was no way he could see." He decided that there is a God. Now, he is a Christian serving the Lord.

Amputate Leg

My husband was shot in an artery. I was told he would not live. That is the first miracle—he did live. The Lord saved him. Then they were going to amputate his leg. It was either above or below the knee. They did not know which location. I called the church, and we all started praying. The next morning, they were going to amputate his leg. The nurse said there was a pulse. Then the operation was cancelled. That was the second miracle.

Crime House

My husband and I were looking for a house to rent. We had four children. We found a two-story with enough rooms for the kids. It was in the area we wanted to live. We decided to put money down. It was $500, which was a lot of money at that time. But I got a bad feeling about the house. I decided to not get the house. My husband was very angry. He said it was perfect for us. I asked the lady for the check back. The next week, I was driving by that house, looking at another house in the neighborhood. It was a crime scene. The person that moved in was murdered. It was next to a park. That would have been me. I would have been alone, answering the door. I would have been killed. To me, that is a miracle.

Poisoned

I hit an eighteen-wheeler two years ago. It was March 26. I stepped out of my totaled pickup truck. I felt pretty good. A week later, I had an ulcer in my stomach as big as my fist. It took ten units of blood to save me. It was a reaction to the dye given during X-rays. The doctor said he thought I had cancer. A month later, all I had was scar tissue. That was a miracle. When I was poisoned two years before, I literally died. I stopped breathing. I was out of the hospital in a week.

I feel like I have gone through several miracles.

I Should Be With You

At the time I was pregnant and working two jobs, I was a food server for one restaurant in the morning and another at night. I was going through a lot. I was a single mother and did not know what to do. I was several hundred miles from my home. I contemplated going home to be with my family. The option of staying weighed on me. You could see the stress on my face about life. I went to work every day without a problem. Then something strange happened one morning as I waited on a table. An older couple asked to speak to me. Actually, it was the lady. They were very nice. Something about her in particular struck me. I could tell she wanted to talk to me before she said anything. She asked what my name was and how I was doing. I was four months pregnant, and nobody knew. You could not tell at that point. She said she has something to tell me. "I do not want to offend you."

I said that I was one of the most open-minded people she would ever meet. I will not be offended. I said, "What is it?"

She held my hand and told me that God wanted to tell me everything was going to be okay. "Any doubts or questions you have will be solved. He is going to provide you with the guidance you need, as long as you ask." I want to remind you, this lady had no idea what I was going through. She did not know who I was, what my story was, nothing about me. They became regular customers after that talk. She gave me little books on the word of God. After we talked a little bit, she became aware of my financial situation. We then built a wonderful relationship. It definitely made an impact on my life.

Knocking

I was with one of my friends. We were riding the bus since my car had broken down. It was really cold that day. We were not prepared for the weather. We were waiting at the bus stop with sleeveless tops. There was a young lady walking to her car. We asked her if we could have a ride. She said yes. Where I was going was five minutes away. I told her we would give her gas money. She said, "No, not a problem." We hopped in the car. She asked what our names were and what we did? At the end of the trip, she said, "I have something to tell you two. I need to tell each of you individually." I said okay. So she talked to my friend. What she said, I do not know.

Then it was my turn. She said, "God wants me to tell you that whatever you are grabbing onto, he wants you to let it go. He said if you let it go, he will send the guidance and direction you have been asking for." She did not know that I had been praying to God about guidance. I was lost. I felt very lost at that time. I felt like the path I was on was a very crooked one. She said I needed to let go of something. She did not know what was being referred to. I was in a troubled relationship. She said, "Your life is looking like this." She did a zigzag pattern with her hand. She said, "You will be sent in the direction you want, if you let go of what you are hanging onto."

It was amazing. After that, she invited me to church. We connected, and I went to her church. But it was too radical for me, and I never attended again. It was not the way I praise God. It was definitely an experience to know that God was listening to my prayers. He was sending answers through people. It was him talking through these people. God said, "I am listening. I am right here knocking on your door."

Trampoline

A miracle happened to me when I was five. I fell off a trampoline. I broke my neck. Thank God I was not paralyzed. I walk fine now.

Rosary

I had an experience that I felt strongly. It was surreal. I had just come back from Italy. I was there for two weeks. We went to Vatican City. It was awesome. I am not a Catholic, but I was born a Catholic. I was raised Catholic till middle school. I do not pray like Catholics pray. I just pray to God. I know that God exists. In the Vatican, I bought a rosary. I dipped it in holy water. I also bought a statue of a woman kissing a child. A Christ follower that was hardcore was talking to me. One day I was touching him, and he said not to touch him. He had gotten a bad spirit from a girl touching him a long time ago. I was offended and hurt. The next day, he said he wanted to apologize for the way he acted. He said he was praying about it. He saw a woman sacrificing her child. He asked if I brought anything back from Italy. At first I said no.

Then I remembered the rosary that I put around the mother in the statue. He said that is exactly what he saw when he was praying. I went home and cast that thing out of my house. I broke it. That was God telling me, "I thought you believed in me." I felt like I was questioning him, not knowing I was questioning him. "I am the only one, not this rosary or shrine. Why are you holding someone in place of me?" I was raised Catholic, and my whole family is Catholic. Sorry if I offended anyone.

No Nurse

A sixteen-year-old girl went to the hospital for a double lung transplant, obviously close to death. The nurse was kind and compassionate and loving. After leaving the hospital, she went back with her family to thank the nurse. The nurse did not exist. She was not a nurse in the hospital. The girl is now a healthy thirty-two-year-old woman.

Motorcycle Deer

When I was eighteen, I wasn't yet walking with Christ. I had gotten on my motorcycle to go to my mother's house. That morning, I was wearing shorts and a light shirt. I had on sunglasses. I did not have a helmet. I was coming around a corner and saw a deer. Despite hitting the brakes, I hit the deer. It literally cut the deer in half. I was going fast. By the grace of God, I stayed with the bike. I slid about sixty or seventy yards. The only thing I could think of was if I stop and am still alive, I had to get up. When I did stop, I picked the bike up. I threw it in the ditch. I could not possibly do that in my right mind. I then walked a half mile to my mom's. She took me to the hospital. We found out later from a state trooper that 90 percent of accidents with a deer, the driver goes over the handlebars. Then they break their neck. To me, it is a miracle that I survived.

Arkansas Golf Cart

I have a ten-year-old cousin. She and a friend were riding a golf cart in the Arkansas country. They were riding around their property. They were riding around in a field. As they crossed a private road, a guy hit them going about sixty miles per hour. There were three kids on the golf cart. My cousin was pronounced dead at the scene. She was taken to a hospital by care flight. She was revived. Today, she is twelve years old. She has had brain surgery four times. Also her spleen and pelvis were ruptured. It only took a year to recover. That was a miracle.

Go Back

My grandpa had recently passed away. He worked in the corn field. The machine that picked corn caught his shirt as he was walking by. He got pulled into the machine. He then passed away in the accident. After this accident happened, he told his granddaughter that was in a bad wreck to go back. "It is not your time." He told her to tell everyone that he loved them and he is fine. In our time, it was hours. In her time, it was five minutes.

Birth 2

I have lots of miracles in my lifetime. My husband and I had been married fourteen years. But we could not have children. We were blessed to finally have a kid. I had another baby after that baby was six months old.

Choking

I was driving one day and started choking. I could not breathe. I pulled over and got out of the car. People thought I was crazy. At that point, I hit my chest really hard. I believe God saved me. I was on the way to the hospital to visit my dad, and it was a scary moment for me.

Kennedy

The last time I saw my father was when President Kennedy came from Lovefield airport. After the president passed, I saw a halo on his head. I also saw colors like I had never seen in my life. Shortly after that, the president was shot. That was the first time I saw my father cry.

Wave

My son and I were on the beach in San Diego, California. We then decided to go out in the ocean. We went out to about waist-high water. Neither of us could swim. The waves were getting kind of crazy. We decided to head back to the shore. As soon as we turned around, the sun was blocked by a big wave. The wave knocked me down. I was holding on to my son. He went completely out of my arms. The water was deeper there. I could not even stand. For whatever reason, he slipped out of my hands. The wave brought him back to me, and I grabbed him. We both came back up. That was a scary moment. You never know. Something was there.

Car Flip

A girl was in a very bad car wreck. The car flipped over three times. She was knocked unconscious. After a time, she regained consciousness. She kicked out the window and got out of the car. Every person around was shocked. Everyone was pretty sure she was dead.

Knee

A man with a shotgun shot a man at close range. He totally missed him. This same man that was shot at had pain in his knee for many years. He had the knee prayed over. The pain persisted for a few days. Then it went away for good.

There was no more pain ever again. That was years ago.

Bunk Bed

A man was in prison. He was told late one night that he was being moved from the east wing to the west wing. For obvious reasons, he was scared. This man was always in prayer. In his new cell, he was lying on the bottom of a bunk bed. Looking up, he saw words on the bottom of the bed above. It said, "Believe and Live, Love Faith and Hope. With God all things are possible. Give thanks joyously. Even during hard times." These words were seen with his spiritual eyes.

Savior

Miracles happen every day. I know I can count on the Lord, and things will be all right. I will have a blessed day. The miracle is to know that our savior lived. We are blessed to be here on earth. That is a miracle to me—to read the scriptures and know my testimony grows day by day. I say this in the name of Jesus Christ.

Four Days Dead

I was involved in a church. A man came to speak that had been dead for four days. Rigor mortis had set in.

He was alive and full of energy. This sounds like Lazarus. Although many will doubt this, remember all things are possible with the lord.

Choking Mom and Fire

About two years ago, there was a situation where I was driving home. I decided to visit one of my friend's mother. It was very rare to see her. She had a stroke in the past. She was doing all right and taking care of herself. Anyway, I was over there visiting. She started choking on some water as she was watching a funny television show. It was not a coincidence that I was there. I started using the Heimlich maneuver. She started breathing again. I said afterward, "Can you imagine if I was not here?" I rarely visit her. That one incident was the time she needed to see me. The very next day, I was driving late at night. I saw a glow in the distance. It was in my neighborhood. I was wondering what it could be. It was real late at night. As I got closer, I could see it was a fire. A house was completely engulfed in flames. I called 911 and asked if the fire had been reported. They said no. Again, I was in the right place at the right time. Some people call this a coincidence. I say, I was there at that exact moment to help somebody out.

First Face

I was fifty-one years old. Every night, I was going on the street. I asked myself, *What am I doing out on the street? What am I looking for?* January 1, 1987, I was at the American Legion. I saw a female. I did not look to see if she was skinny or fat. It did not make any difference. I just saw her face. Did you hear the song by Roberta Flack titled "The First Time Ever I Saw Her Face"? That was real. The person who had written that must have had an experience like I did. I did not do anything right away. I was getting my nerves up. I asked her to dance. We talked, and the words came so easy. I said to myself, *This is what I have been looking for.* She was my miracle.

Two-Year Dream

In 2012, my grandmother passed away. She was living in Mexico. After almost two years, she came back on my birthday in my dreams. She told me that she loves me.

She wanted to say happy birthday. I did not want her to leave. She gave me a kiss and said good-bye. She was wearing white. I did not want to wake up from my dream, but at least I got to see her.

Blood Pressure

I was in the hospital. I had high blood pressure. It was 250 over 100 and something. The doctor said I would not live that night. The blood vessels in my brain were about to explode. I had my whole family around me. Everybody was crying, waiting for me to pass away. They could not bring my blood pressure down. For some odd reason, I woke up the next morning. That is a miracle. I should have been very dead. I am fine now.

A Pastor's Testimony

This is a testimony from a pastor. I would like to start by saying that I am truly grateful for another opportunity to tell how God started a relationship with me. Also, how that relationship has developed where I can sincerely say that God spoke to me and commanded me to preach the gospel to his people. With this in mind, I would like to describe and explain my understanding of this very important call to serve. In doing so, I must reveal brief experiences of my past, to clarify my belief. Following this, I will discuss how one day I became desperate enough to have a meaningful conversation with the Lord. From that day, I can truly say that God is real. His mercy endures forever. Upfront, I confess that I neither deserve nor am I worthy of the special attention God has given me. However, because I am fully convinced of his will for my life, I accept the conditions of this calling and embrace the responsibilities associated with it. Without further delay, please allow me to share the life changing convictions of my life.

First of all, I would like to say that I have always felt an obligation to do what is right and just. Needless to say, I was introduced to Jesus Christ at a very early age. I received my early Christian education in Arkansas at a church. I do not remember a great deal about my initial experience. However, I do recall being sincere in acknowledging that I was a sinner. I seemingly understood the consequences of my sin. Therefore, I asked for forgiveness and accepted Jesus Christ as my Lord and Savior. Afterward, I was baptized.

With the peace in knowing that I was going to heaven one day, I primarily based my belief on what other people said or how they lived. And like many others, I never matured as a believer of Jesus Christ. This was due to the fact that I never read the Bible for myself. I did not listen very well when the word of God was being preached. Consequently, my understanding about living saved was very distorted. Before long, I found myself getting drunk and committing fornication as a teenager. Although I professed to be a Christian, this behavior was considered normal in my environment. Drinking liquor was not a big deal for me either. After all, I had heard that even Jesus turned water into wine. Lying came easy as well. Plus I knew ushers and choir members who went to church and supported the local nightclub! I can remember smelling liquor on their breath as they sang on Sunday mornings.

I could go on and on. I could blame any number of people for my lack of commitment to God. I can't remember anyone strongly objecting to the lifestyle I had chosen. After leaving home, I quit attending church services. I spent Sunday's doing what I wanted to do. I didn't have a relationship with the Lord, nor was I seeking him for guidance. Daily decisions were based on my own experiences and what I understood I had to do to survive. I enjoyed the freedom of doing what I wanted to do, saying what I wanted to say, and going where I wanted to go. Yet I was not happy, and I didn't feel loved. I was in and out of relationships. I knew something was missing in my life, and I felt empty and meaningless inside. Strangely enough, I always remembered to pray. After all, I believed in Jesus Christ. But I was certainly not living according to the scriptures.

This self-righteousness continued until one day I began to realize God was too good to me. Suddenly, I was aware of his righteousness compared to my unrighteousness. I became fearful and felt I didn't have much time left on this earth. So I began to talk to God about my problems. The longer I talked, the more real the conversation became. I desperately needed some answers. Suddenly, I became sorrowful for the many sins I had committed before God. I became even more aware of my sinful condition and began to pray for mercy from a loving God. Afterward, I began to feel a sense of peace and joy asking God to help.

For the first time, I felt the true love of God. He saved a wretch like me! From that day, I made a commitment to know God and what he expected of me. I began to study the Bible and attend church services. I had a new hunger and thirst for righteousness. The anger I used to keep inside was no longer there. I found myself in situations that were very uncomfortable. For example, I was at a nightclub one night and witnessed a man put a gun on the side of a young lady's head. I recall closing my eyes and walking out of the club. The more I heard the word of God, the stronger my Christian walk became.

As a result of my relationship with God, I asked my wife to marry me. For the first time, I wanted to do what was right in the relationship. Just to think, God cared enough about me to allow his only son to die for me. I felt a growing sense of loyalty to God. I found myself telling my close friends and relatives about the change in my life. Some were happy, while others didn't know what to think. I also found myself urging others and to turn from a life of wickedness.

As I recall, my first real audience was at my family reunion in July of 1993. I can't remember everything I said, but I do remember encouraging them to repent and surrender to Jesus Christ. My intent was to introduce Jesus Christ to some and stir up the Holy Spirit in others. After speaking, I cried tears of joy for the first time in my life! Even then, I did not sense a call on my life. I shared the gospel with my family members, because I wanted them to be free of the bondage of sin and experience the joy that salvation brings. Since that day, my father, two brothers, and my youngest sister have turned from a life of sin. Of course, this didn't happen overnight. As a matter of fact, it took approximately five years. Nevertheless, I am thankful that God called them out of a life of darkness into a life of love and peace.

After the family reunion, I caught a flight and departed for South Korea to spend one year away from my new and pregnant wife. Somehow, I knew this separation would be the first challenge to our marriage. As expected, I encountered many temptations. However, my relationship with God allowed me to resist every time. My stay in Korea was a humbling experience. I literally worked every day from sunup to sundown. I was assigned to a protocol office where I washed dishes and opened doors for dignitaries. I carried luggage, organized seminars, arranged dinner engagements, and went shopping with our special guests. My job required me to smile and move quickly, regardless of how I felt about the task. I followed a daily agenda, which required me to manage my time wisely. To my amazement, I enjoyed my duties most of the time. Little did I know, this was my initial training in serving the public as a minister.

Being without my wife allowed me to spend significant time to pray and study the word of God. As a result, my relationship with God was strengthened even more. After returning from South Korea, I arrived home to exercise my duties as a husband and a father of our lovely little daughter. Needless to say, I was not ready for such a huge responsibility. I knew the word of God; however, I did not exercise wisdom in applying Godly principles to my life. For instance, I was quick to let my wife know that I was head of the house. Therefore, she needed to submit to me. Before I realized what was happening, I was overwhelmed and started to withdraw from my wife and God.

After a year of frustration and bitter arguments with my wife, I began to allow ungodly influences in my life. I had given up on my marriage and returned to a world of sinfulness. However, God had a different plan for my family and me. One morning, after a major argument, my wife and I decided to get a divorce. I recall going to work, and suddenly the Holy Spirit began to remind me of my commitment to God. I had to decide whether to submit to God's righteousness or trust in my own evil desires. Immediately, I repented and asked God to help me. Next, I called my wife and told her I did not know how we were going to make it; however, I was confident that the Lord would show us the way. She agreed, and we began to pray for God to lead us to a church where the truth was being preached. Also, where we could be ministered to as a family.

To be brief, God led us to a Holiness Church where I learned to worship God on a new level. I found myself studying the Bible and seeking God even more. Then it happened! One night, while the preacher was preaching, I looked up toward the pulpit and sensed a strong presence of God. I wanted to run and touch the "hem of his garment." Somehow, I knew God was present, and to touch that preacher would give me the blessing I so desperately needed. Reluctantly, I kept my seat and waited.

After the preacher was done, a prayer line was formed. Anyone desiring a blessing from God was asked to come forward. Of course I leaped out of my seat and walked toward the preacher. For the first time in worship service, I didn't care if anyone was looking at me or what anyone thought of my actions. My primary concern was to be blessed by God. When the oil was placed on my forehead, I recall speaking in tongues. Immediately, my legs weakened, and I fell to the floor. While I was on that floor, God spoke to me and said, "Go forth and preach my word." God knew my thoughts and spoke the same words again to me. I responded by saying, "Yes, Lord." After which, there was a long silence. Then, God spoke again and said, "Do not depart from me."

Before I could answer, he made the same statement again. Knowing others would doubt this experience, God gave me a scripture (Matthew 9:10) to confirm to me and all present that he was speaking to me. I rose to my feet, and found myself still praising God. I knew I had to inform the church. I told the congregation that God had called me to preach the gospel. Furthermore, I gave them the scripture that God had given me to give to them. I must add that when I gave the scripture to the congregation, I had no idea that such a scripture existed. However, once I gave it to them, there was no turning back.

Since that night, I have faithfully preached the gospel to many people. By the grace of God, I have led many more to salvation. Now I understand why as a child, I stepped on a snake and was not bitten. I fell over twelve feet backward out of a tree and landed beside a huge rock. No bones were broken. I survived a major car accident (a broken jaw, a fractured collarbone, a congestive heart failure, and a collapsed right lung). Needless to say, I am convinced that God has a special purpose for me!

When Paul talks about the way God brings salvation into our lives, he says, "Those whom he predestined, he also called; and those whom he had called he also justified; and those whom he justified, he also glorified" (Romans 8:30). Here Paul points to a definite order in which the blessings of salvation come to us. Paul also indicates that calling is an act of God. In fact, it is specifically an act of God the father. He is the one who predestines people to "be conformed to the image of his son" (Romans 8:29). God's calling has the capacity to draw people out of the kingdom of darkness and bring them into God's kingdom so they can join in full fellowship with him. "God is faithful, by whom you were called into the fellowship of his son, Jesus Christ our Lord" (1 Corinthians 1:9).

At this time, my specific calling is in the prison ministry. I have ministered to prisoners for over four years and been actively involved in outdoor worship services. Both of these activities combine to effectively seek and minister to lost souls, whether in confinement of prison or on the community streets. My mission is simple—to exhort, assist, and equip the church in its ministry to prisoners, ex-prisoners, victims and their families, and in its advancement of Biblical standards of justice.

I have received my formal training in in-prison ministry, family ministry, and aftercare ministry. Subjects included were problems faced by prisoners, ex-prisoners and their families, helping skills, and prison fellowship programs. Additionally, I have been cleared to visit any prison in Texas. Furthermore, I have conducted over five hundred hours in individual counseling and group services in the local community and abroad. Currently, I am pursuing a religious education degree from Wayland Baptist University. As I stated earlier, I am married. My wife's name is Veronica. We have one beautiful daughter and two handsome sons.

Baseball Tournament

In my freshman year in college, we had a rough season in baseball. We got to play in the playoffs anyway. We played in the conference tournament. We were the last-place team. Then we won six straight games in the college world series. Then we won four games and the national championship. We were the first last-place team in junior college history to win a national championship.

Just for the record, I am too big to wear my ring; it does not fit anymore.

Backpack

A man went to Asia. He was in Thailand. He had all of his belongings in a backpack. He fell asleep riding on a bus. His backpack was stolen, and he was in a real bad position. He did not speak the language. After searching in vain, a cab driver who spoke limited English said, "Come with me." He went and got his backpack back. The odds were staggering of ever getting it back.

Three Years in a Car

After I got out of the Air Force, I lived in my car for three years. Then my car got repossessed, and I was living in different friends' houses. I went from house to house. God blessed me with a basic job, working at a gas station. I moved in with my cousin. Then, I met my wife to be. I went to work at a warehouse. It was a pay increase, and my life got a little better. I was able to buy a car. From there, I attended a private school.

I enjoyed that for four years. I gave that up because they desired somebody else. I went eleven months without a job. My wife had a baby, and the baby had seizures. Now my family is in a position that I can get pretty much what they want. Looking back to where I came from, to where I am now has been an amazing blessing. Only God could do it.

Sixteen

When I was sixteen, I got very sick. I went through many treatments with no success. I became completely well with no explanation.

Hand

A lady's husband died. She was lying in bed with her hands crossed. She felt a hand on top of her hand. Perhaps it was the comforter. She definitely was comforted by the incident.

RPG

I was serving in Iraq. An RPG impacted a wall right behind me. It did not explode. About fifteen minutes later, we moved out. We heard a loud explosion behind us. It went off. Of course, I am still here. It is a miracle that I was not killed.

MD

I have a nine-year-old son. My wife carries the muscular dystrophy gene. She had two brothers pass away from that disease. My wife carries it, but does not have it. My wife could potentially have a child with the disease. We were married ten years in fear of having a kid. If we had a daughter, she would not get MD. However she would have the same situation when she grew up. After ten years, we decide to have a child. We felt that we could handle any result. We took that chance, with no adverse effects.

Behind Curtain

This world is truly amazing and blessed. People everywhere do not take the time to realize how blessed they are. That is the difference between people who are successful and stuck in a rut. You have to look behind the curtain. When you think outside the box, there are no limits. Faith in God is what creates belief in yourself. There is a difference in thinking and knowing. My dad passed away nine years ago, and my mom had open heart surgery that same year. Realizing you are gifted because of God, that is when your life changes. Your father that gave you life and your mother are not your true parents. When you realize your only true father is God, Jesus, that is when you realize that your gift is life-changing. People may tell you, you are good at this or that—painting, football, baseball, skateboarding, snowboarding, and so on. It all does not matter.

It took me awhile to realize that I am very talented. The reason I finally realized it was God. I am part of something bigger than these things. It is in the book of life. Understanding that is what makes people know why they are here. You must open the curtain and look outside the box. It is all a blessing, something you are ordained to be. We all have it. A lot of people never realize it. You either do or you don't; there is no trying. It is not what you say; it is what you do.

MPH Wreck

When I was in high school, my friend hit a tree going about eighty miles per hour. The car flipped vertical over a cow pasture fence without knocking it down. The car landed against another tree in a vertical position. Neither of us had even a scratch.

Park Predator

I was in the fifth grade, living in Rochelle, Illinios. My brother and I were riding our bikes ahead of my parents in a park. For some reason, I told my brother that I did not want him at the park with me. I didn't understand why. I knew that he should not be there with me. I went on to the playground. I noticed a gentleman lingering by the park. Fortunately there was another family at the playground. Well, they soon left. Being a ten-year-old boy, I was still subject to the fears of not knowing strangers. You do not know what is going on.

I heard a voice say, "You need to walk away." There was nobody there, but I heard, "You need to walk away." So I started making my way away from the playground. I find my mother and brother. My brother was not happy with me for obvious reasons. I told her that there was something very odd going on. I returned to the spot on the playground with her. That man was standing there, staring at me. I knew there was something wrong. Somebody was looking out for me.

December Rain

On December 21 this last year, I had to drive five hours away to Alpine, Texas. My car was in the shop, so I took my son's car. It was a Honda Civic. I drove, and night was approaching. My wife wanted me to stay there, because it was getting dark and raining. There was a storm coming in. I left Alpine at about 10:00 p.m. It was pouring down rain, and it was really windy. A lot of that stretch of highway was separated by a ravine. I was travelling eighty miles per hour, and the car started to hydroplane. A huge semi-eighteen-wheeler passed me and sprayed the car. I lost control and twisted around twice. It threw me backward. There was a level grassy median that I crossed over. There were trucks coming at me. I had the good sense to step on the gas. I got back on the median. There is absolutely no reason why I should be alive today. I got out of the car. My car and I were both fine. I said a little thankful prayer to God. I was so disoriented. I was just waiting for the blows and injury. That is all I was waiting for. It rained and stormed all the way back. I crawled back slowly. I got back at five o'clock in the morning. Of course, I got scolded by my wife. She said, "You should have stayed there and waited for the storm to pass." But I was so much of a knucklehead that I came all the way back. To me, that was truly miraculous. Under the circumstances, the car would have been severely damaged. I would have been knocked off the highway. I would have been severely injured or dead. Nothing happened, except for the knowledge that I was being protected by someone a lot stronger than anyone.

Emphysema

Fifteen years ago, I was diagnosed with severe emphysema. I have since been taking a large amount of vitamins and herbs. Now there are no traces of emphysema. I have a little bit of asthma, but no emphysema.

2 Percent

I was in a car accident in 2009. I had a 2 percent survival chance. It was when I was late for school and got hit by an eighteen-wheeler. I went straight into a coma. It lasted for two months, but I recovered. I had to learn how to walk again, read again, and learn math again. I had to relearn everything. I just graduated from college. I became a phlebotomist—I open a vein to remove or release blood.

10 Percent

My cousin was born three months premature. The doctors gave him a less than 10 percent chance of survival. He is thirteen years old now, and I consider him to be a miracle.

Family

The biggest miracle for me, I would say, is my family. I am so glad to have them. My sister just had a baby girl. As common as that is, it was a miracle to me. I will not be here much longer. I will soon be in the military. My miracle now is being here while I can.

Rectal

My mom was diagnosed with rectal cancer and ovarian cancer about twenty-five years ago. She was given six months to live. She is now eighty. Totally cancer-free, and no doctor can explain why.

Purpose

One day, I was coming down the highway. I was just driving, my head in the air. I knew God had been talking to me, but I would ignore him. I was not paying attention to God. I know he had a purpose for me in life. That was to talk to people for him. I was about to have an accident at an intersection. Just as I was about to go into the intersection, God woke me up. He showed me that I needed to swerve. I said, "All right, Lord, I hear you." From that day on, I started living for him. I lived my life for his purpose. From that point, he would talk to me to tell people what I was here for. He would tell me things, that I could give my voice to him. Things I would say from him were true. My grandchildren would tell me not to tell them what God said, because they always came true. From then on, I had to say what God said. There were times when I wouldn't. He would admonish me and ask why I did not talk when I could. I stopped that.

Bus Men

About four years ago, I was at a bus stop waiting for my bus. I was waiting for number 4 bus. Two guys were walking toward me. They looked like rabbis. One started looking at me, then both looked at me. I looked behind me to see if someone was there. They got on my bus, and sat in the front. One kept looking at me and pointed his finger toward me. It was really spooking me. I got up and sat on the other side by a lady. Then I noticed a fence in the direction they came from. I asked myself how they could have come from that direction. All of a sudden he looked at me and said, "Don't go to Israel, my child."

I looked at him and said, "Are you talking to me?"

He said, "Yes, my child. Come and sit by me, and I will tell you."

I said, "All right." It seemed like nobody paid any attention about me talking to this old man.

He looked straight into my eyes, and said, "My child, you are given God's blessing. I am telling you, something is going to take place in Israel. Do not go to Israel." (This was March 1, 2014.)

I said, "I do not have the money to go to Israel."

He said, "Things are going to change real quick. God is going to bless you, because you are one of the chosen ones." They rang the bell and got off the bus. I looked where they had to be; they had disappeared. I never forgot that. I told my friend about it. She said she had the same experience in a church. "After everyone left, I was still sitting down in the pew. A guy tapped me on the shoulder. I looked over there, and he said, 'You are a Christian, aren't you?' He said my name.

"I said, 'How do you know my name? You are not a regular person in this church.'

"'No, I am not. God is going to give you a blessing soon. It is what you have been asking for.'" She went home and told her husband what had happened. About three months later, she got the low-cost housing she had been praying for. She never saw that guy again.

Miscarriage

My mother was told by twenty-seven doctors that she would never have kids. Finally, a doctor said he believes anything is possible. He said there is a slim chance for her to have kids. She had four miscarriages and two children.

My brother and I are surviving miracles.

$80,000

My dad passed away, and I got a check for eighty thousand dollars. I stayed the same, but my so-called friends changed. They stole from me and broke into my account. I started a business club. Somehow, they knew about it. They broke into my house and stole everything I bought with the money. They lied to my boss. They told him I was doing drugs. Then I almost became homeless. The power was shut off in my home, and I ended up moving in with my mom. I then moved four hundred miles away. My life has gotten better. That was my miracle.

Stomach Pains

In 2009, I was having stomach pains. I was not too sure what was going on. I told my husband about it. He said, "Don't worry about it." He said to just stay at home. I had no health insurance. The stomach pain got progressively worse. It got to the point that if I stood up, I would be in fear of falling down. I was not sure what was going on. It was so bad, I had to go to the emergency room at the hospital. They took me in and found I had a ruptured fallopian tube. I had a baby in there. I had been bleeding internally for two weeks. The one doctor who could do that procedure was at the hospital. The odds against that were very high. He did it robotically. This whole event saved my life. I would have bled to death. The doctor removed the baby from the fallopian tube, and I am here now because of it.

Out of Control

A car was speeding toward me out of control. A woman was trying to control it as I was trying to cross the street. It all happened so fast, I had no time to react. Somebody took my hand and got me out of trouble. I know it was not my doing. I know it was God. I lived through it.

Chapel

I am thankful for the miracle that God did for me. It happened in the chapel. Basically, I had lost a lot of money. It was important to me. I thought that life was all about money. But it was not true. It is about God. When I lost the money, I felt like that was the end of the world. I was really sick. I could not function or sleep. I had to try to live some more. I was scared. There was no true value to that money. I knew that on the inside. It does not last. You can't take it with you when you go. You have to be happy with what God gives you. Blessings and grace are more important than anything else. I was invited to an ash retreat. That was when I was at my sickest point. It was the second day about five, and we were going into the chapel. I started crying profusely. I followed the others in. I sat down in the fifth row. I kept crying. I could not stop.

There was a pot broken. Each person got a piece of that pot. We were told to leave all of our baggage and put the piece we had into an unbroken pot. I did that and returned to my seat. I sat down and prayed. I was still crying, and all of a sudden, I felt a tingling above my head. It was all peaceful. There was no more crying or worry. I stopped taking prescribed drugs, and I slept well. I started attending church on a regular basis. I still enjoy making money, but that is not what I value anymore. The true value is God. Church is why we are here, meeting people of like minds. We are not there to make money. That is not it.

Waste Management

Back in February of 2006, I was working for waste management. I was working with a young kid in a subdivision. He was driving, which should have never happened. He stopped abruptly and knocked me pretty bad. I busted my glasses. I saw a lady across the street. Barely conscious, I asked for an icepack. I was in the hospital for fourteen days with a concussion. Six months following, I was in rehab. I had surgery done to my cervical area. That took another twenty-two days. I have been hurting since then. I was in another accident. I was driving a motor coach. A driver slammed into it. It caused me more aggravation to my back and neck. I am now disabled and unable to work. But I am still alive.

Explosion

My parents live in Florida near a propane filling station. It blew up with a huge explosion. My mom suffers from dementia. She is very religious and prays a lot. She always stops at a gas station next to the propane place. She parks in the same spot. She always gets a Dr. Pepper and Snickers bar. That night before the propane explosion, she was driving home. A deer jumped out in front of her car. She hit the deer, and it died. She called animal control. The propane tank blew up. It destroyed the side of the gas station where she parks. She always sits there in the car, eating her candy bar. The tragedy of the deer saved her life. Two underground propane tanks blew up. She definitely attributes that to the man upstairs. It was not a coincidence. She was upset about the deer, but she really feels she was touched by the Lord. Things happen for a reason.

Think God

I was driving home late one night. It was about 2:00 a.m. Usually, I want to get home quickly. As soon as the light turns green, I am off. I do not know why, but I stayed at a light for a second. If I had not waited, I would have been T-boned by a car running the light at about sixty miles per hour. Soon as I got on the freeway, the "Think God" billboard caught my eye.

Water Blaster

God works miracles every day. My miracle began when I was working on a plant. They called me into work on Saturday. I really did not want to go. I was working on a sermon to preach on Sunday. So I went to work anyway.

I was a water blaster. The job was to clean the inside of a large tank. So when I got inside the tank, I was still thinking about the sermon I was going to preach about. As I was in the spirit going over my sermon, I saw some white clouds in the tank with me. I did not understand what they were. As I went over my sermon, I felt the ground move. I did not know what was going on. The plant had blown up. The tank I was in was a nitroglycerin tank. It did not blow up. I realized what I thought were white clouds were angels protecting me. The survivors in the plant thought I was dead. Only by the grace of God was I alive. I was breathing fresh air from an oxygen tank.

When the oxygen tank ran out, a bell rang to let the people know there was no more air in the oxygen tank. I took the mask off. I was still breathing like I had fresh air. God sustained me in the nitroglycerin tank. The second miracle came when I was working in another plant. I had to go three hundred feet in the air. Of course I wore a harness. I had to get in a water tower. It had fans in it. We tagged and locked the fans to the off position. Someone went back and took the locks off. I am sitting inside the tower with a fan above me. There were many fans below me. The total was about twenty-five. I was sitting on a fan blade, water blasting another fan blade below me. I was thanking and praising God.

I was singing a song. It was "I have been on the battlefield for a long time." As I was singing that song, I happened to look down. One of the blades under me was coming on. I looked up, another blade on top of me was turning on. I was saying, "Lord, they can't turn the power on, because they know I am in here." Only by the grace of God was my life spared. All of the fans were supposed to come on. The one I was sitting on did not. Neither did the one below me. See how God is. The power just skipped over the fan I was on. The people were yelling for me. They thought I was dead. By the time they got three hundred up and looked inside, I was still there. Miracle, God will protect you. That is my miracle.

Memory Gift

I got a gift from God. I was two years old. I remember the 23rd Psalm. At four years old, I remember a booklet of Psalms. I have a miracle of memory from the age of two to the age of forty-nine. I can remember every pastor, every scripture, everything I had done since the age of two. Every place I lived, all my school teachers, all my schools. It was a gift from God—to know his words, every passage in the Bible. God gives gifts. I am fortunate to have one. Only may God love you. May he keep you and bless you.

Bouncing Tree

I had a situation happen. In the military, my friends and I were clearing out some brush and tree trunks. Four of us were carrying a twelve-foot-long tree trunk. It weighed over three hundred pounds. I was on the back. I was not paying attention when we all agreed to put it on our left shoulder to toss it over. I had it on my right shoulder. Every other person had it on the left. When we went to toss it, I tried to lift it over my head as they released the tree trunk. The tree fell to the ground and bounced into my neck. I was knocked out. I remember saying, "Oh, Jesus. Oh, Jesus. Oh, Jesus." I know God protected me!

End Poverty

I lived on the street for ten years. I was living in Seattle, Washington. Sleepless in Seattle. God told me to give up all I had, and I did. I got approved by the military. They gave me $38,000. I get $3,000 every month. I am now in a house on Gabriel Street. I was finally off the street. Thank God. It was hard living with raccoons, snakes, and ants. I have a website called "Can We End Poverty." Somebody, please help me tell my story to the world.

Niagara Falls

This next miracle reminds me of the angel with lot.

This was over twenty years ago. I went to Niagara Falls to have some personal time. I went there with the intention of staying three days. I was in my room praying and fasting, only drinking water. I was spending time with the Lord, only talking to him. I got on the *Maid of the Mist*. I had a great time. I had a great dinner. I took the bus back home. That was the first and last time I would take a bus. It was a lot of miles from Buffalo to Baltimore. My husband was in the military in Saudi Arabia at the time. I figured I would be fine on the bus. The bus arrived in New York City at 2:00 a.m. I was dropped off at the end of the terminal. The bus I needed to catch was at the other end. It is a huge bus terminal.

So at 2:00 a.m., I was walking in the New York bus station. I could hear the *click, click, click* of my luggage. I asked the attendant where to go. I did not know it, but two young teenagers were following me. I think their intention was to rob me. Of course, I am not sure. A short old woman comes up to me. She said, "Hey, how are you doing?"

I said, "Fine." We started talking. I told her my husband was deployed. I was having some time off. We were talking and walking. I said, "Hey look, there is an elevator." I got on the elevator. The two young men that were following me got on the elevator.

The lady looked at me and said, "Let's keep walking." When I went to get off the elevator, the two young men blocked my way. She said come with me. When she motioned, the two young men fell to the side of the elevator. They could not move. I was just looking at them. I wondered if they were okay. I looked at her, and she said, "Come on, sweetheart." I said okay. It was really weird. She said, "You need to be more careful about where you go."

I said, "Yes, ma'am, I will." That was the last thing she said to me. She disappeared. I was looking for her everywhere. She had said she was going to Washington, DC. I looked on that bus for her. But I could not find her. I was riding on the bus before I became aware of what just happened. She saved my life. It wasn't till the next morning that I realized the full gravity of the situation. That was my guardian angel.

Gall Bladder

I had surgery a couple years ago to remove my gall bladder. There was a man admitted to the hospital with cancer. He said he had been told three times that he had cancer. The doctor said, "So you are a walking miracle."

He said, "No, I just have faith."

Cancer Not Found

Two years ago, I went to the doctor and was told I have cancer. They did a needle biopsy but found nothing. I felt like a ton of bricks hit my head. I told my wife about it. I asked, "What am I supposed to do now?" I was depressed, waiting to pass away. I thought there was a time limit. I did not know how long. The doctor said I needed to keep coming. I was scared. When I saw the other people at the hospital, I thought, *Oh my God*. They looked at me, which scared me more. I did not know how advanced I was. I just live day by day. I feel it in my body, and I smell it. I have not received any medication or treatment. To me, that is a divine message.

1979

In 1979, I had a miracle happen to me. I received a call that my dad was in the hospital. I was told he was real sick. He probably would not make it. I lived two hundred miles away. I had an old car. I had just gotten out of the service. I was in the Marine Corps. I was driving as fast as I could to see my dad alive. My car stopped from heating up. It got so hot, I could not get it started again. As I was waiting there, a big yellow car stopped behind me. A man asked, "What is the problem?"

I said, "My car does not start. It is overheated." I said, "I need some water."

He said, "I have three gallons."

I said to myself, *What a coincidence.* He gave me a gallon of water. I said, "Thank you, I appreciate it." I poured water in the radiator. The car started gurgling, like someone real thirsty. The guy told me to calm down.

He said, "The car is going to start, and you will take off."

I was thinking to myself, *How does he know the car will start?* I figured the engine block was probably cracked. I asked him how far he was going. He said he was going far away. He took off. I waited a few more minutes. The car started like he said it would. I was surprised. I tried to calm down, like he said. I wanted to see my dad before he passed away. When I got to the hospital, I told my wife what happened. Then I told my sister and mom. They said it was my guardian angel.

Bad Eyes

I wanted to say what the Lord has done for me, besides salvation. The miracles that he has worked in my life. I was in prison. My eyes were bad, and I was going blind. I could not see anything except halos. Everything was a haze. I could not see anything. It was sin eating away at my eyes. Before I was sent to prison, my eyes began to get totally red. They were blood red. I felt a lot of pain in my eyes. I was sent to prison for six years. I started crying out to the Lord. I did not know who the Lord was. I did not know that Jesus is our savior. So I started praying to a God that I did not know. Then one night, I was listening to the radio. I heard the message of the cross. I was listening to the Gospel.

I got on my knees on the floor. I asked God to forgive me. I asked Jesus Christ to come into my heart. I was saved there. I started praying for healing of my eyes. I was so scared being in prison, not being able to see. I could not get any medical attention. I knew the Lord could heal. I prayed for help. I finally went to the doctor in prison after six months. He said I needed to come back at least once a month. The Lord did heal my eyes. After release from prison, I did not do anything for my eyes for three years. At my mom's urging, I went to see an eye specialist. I knew the Lord had healed me. The doctor looked into my eyes. He also looked at my record. He said there should be some scarring or tearing with everything that has been going on with your eyes. But he said, "Your eyes are completely fine. There is nothing wrong with your eyes."

I said, "I know, Jesus healed me." Of course he did not believe me. The Lord delivered me out of alcohol, smoking, and a prison gang. I have been blessed. Never lacking anything, I have been able to pay my own way for everything. The Lord has always provided jobs and money. I have paid for my car and insurance. Gas is never a problem. I have done all my parole. Completed all the classes and stipulations. God healed my eyes. The biggest miracle was saving me. The old man is dead and gone. My old ways and habits are dead. I am a new man in Christ. I live for Jesus.

Good Morning

This is a story about a friend of mine. He lived in New York City. He is a happy guy, a wonderful person. In New York, people walk by, and they don't say hi to each other. Walking in a crowd, he looked at a face. For a second, he thought it was somebody familiar. As he got closer, he realized he did not know the person. When he got closer, he noticed the guy looking at him. He said good morning to the guy with a smile. The other guy stopped and said good morning. A few months went by. My friend and I were sitting in the subway. We were sitting next to each other. There was another guy sitting next to him. It happened to be the guy he said good morning to. The guy grabbed his arm and said, "Do you know what you did to me?"

My friend said, "Do I know you?"

He said, "Yes. We were walking months ago, and you said good morning."

My friend said, "I don't recall. You do not remember a person you said good morning to months ago."

The man said he was going to the building where he worked. He was going to the top to commit suicide. "You saying good morning stopped me from doing that." If that didn't happen right in front of me, I would not have believed it. I said to myself, *Really?* It shows you how we are all connected. The smallest things we do affect people. I could not believe good morning was a matter of life and death.

Serious Issues

This is an insight on what I go through each day. I was a drug addict for twelve years. I was on meth and weed. I have been through some serious issues because of that. I have been hit by cars, in a coma, and hit by a lot of things over the years. Inflictions were all over me. I put my family through torture. At the end of the day, I thank God for the well-being of my family. I have had fingers chopped off. I have had legs cut open. I have fallen out of trucks, trees, and cars. After all this, I thank God that I am healthy.

Marines

My son-in-law was in the infantry. He was in the marines in Afghanistan. He has only been out less than a year. I truly believe that prayer had a lot to do with this. I do not remember what the situation was or what their intentions were. He stepped right smack on top of an improvised explosive device. It blew him straight up into the air. He came back down and lived to talk about it. He did not lose any limbs. He heard God's voice tell him to get up. That is a miracle!

Cherry Trees

I have had an interesting life. My husband was a college professor. I was his secretary. We went to Ruidoso, New Mexico. This was after retirement. We decided we wanted to do something. Just sitting in our rocking chairs was not fulfilling. The Robert Frost poem about cherry trees inspired us. So that was what we were going to do. We decided to grow cherry trees. All the locals said they would not grow there. They said, "You have to be crazy. Cherries will not grow here." We were going to prove them wrong. We planted thirty cherry trees. The birds and the frost got them. The birds pecked every cherry. After failing, we had to admit they were right. Anyway, my husband loves raspberries. So we decided to grow raspberries. We planted one row. They did so well, the neighbors asked if we would plant a row for them. We ended up with twelve acres of raspberries. That is a lot of raspberries. It was a terrific success. God blessed it. I just know he did. We did that for twelve years. People came from all over, because the raspberries did so well. We said, "We cannot do this anymore. We are too old. What do we do now?" We decided to think about it overnight. We compared notes in the morning. We both had the same message. It was "go plant raspberries for someone that needs it." We ended up in Mexico. There, we were helping Indians. They were treated terribly. We helped them complete a school. They were going in log cabins. We helped build a nice school building, with a place to live. They had been living in one-room shacks. The floor was dirt. There was a dorm upstairs for the kids to stay. That has been so blessed. It was a wonderful experience. I visited every chance I got. Now, I am too old.

Houston to Africa

My friend from Houston went to Africa. He was a geophysicist. These were trips as a missionary. This trip was far from civilization. He got there with advance notice he was coming. There were 1,100 people that heard he was coming. They were all black, and he was white. They had all the sick people ready to greet and heal them. They asked for prayerful healing. So my friend said, "I do not do that kind of thing. I am more of a conservative person." They were all shocked. They responded that he needed to do that out of necessity.

He said, "All right, it will not do any harm if we pray." The first person came to him. He asked, "What is your problem?" Not exactly low key.

The guy said, "I cannot walk. Look at my legs."

He said, "All right, now be quiet. I am going to pray." So he prayed for the guy. Suddenly, the guy stood up and walked. Another person sits down. In his direct way, he said, "What is your problem?"

"I am blind."

He said, "All right, I do not want to hear the details. Bow your head, and I will pray." He healed and saved a bunch of people. He did not think too much about it. Driving home, he argued with God. He felt uncomfortable doing all that. He said, "I get it. Pray for healing is part of the program now. Just do not tell the people back in the States what I am doing. My supporters are going to freak out." He said what happened was the norm. It was not what we did. It was the miraculous.

BMW

Two weeks ago, I was in an addiction treatment program. Twelve steps, not alcohol but gambling. I went in and learned about the twelve steps. I wanted out of the program. I was torn because of my addiction. I woke up Wednesday morning, after getting out of the program that weekend. I heard a commercial about cars. So I applied, even though I did not feel I could afford it. Lo and behold, I drove a BMW off the lot that day. The twelve steps actually says that if you do turn things over to God, things will happen. This was a miracle.

I got Christ in my life in 1995. My life changed quite a bit. I am a disabled veteran. I got a new home. I got married to a wonderful wife, who is an attorney. We live the blessed life. That is my miracle.

Hawaii Coral

My husband and I went to Hawaii. He decided to go out in the water of the ocean. He was caught in a riptide. It was dragging him out. I knew his life was in God's hands. I am elderly and watched helplessly. All of a sudden, a little Hawaiian girl on a surfboard came up to him. She said, "Sir, you are in trouble." She put him on the surfboard and got him back to shore. She then disappeared. He never saw her again. Apparently, he had many coral wounds on his feet. We bought some Kopua oil. Within three weeks, the wounds were gone. No marks were left. Most people take a year to heal from coral.

Purpose on Life

One day I was driving down the highway. I knew God was speaking to me, but I would just ignore him. I came to an intersection. I was not paying attention to God. I know he has a purpose for me in life. It was to talk to people for him. I came into the intersection not aware of what I was doing. I swerved, and said alright Lord, I hear you. From that day on, I started living for him. From then on, God would talk to people about what I am here for. I said things through him to my grandchildren. They would tell me, granny, don't say any more. Everything I said came true. From that point, I had to tell what God told me. When I tried to deny God, he would ask why. I had to give it up.

Took Hand

A car was speeding toward me out of control. The driver tried to control the car, but could not. I was trying to process what was happening. Somebody took my hand, and took me to safety. I know it was not my doing. I know it was God. That is all there is to it.

Honduras

I was sitting at my desk, trying to plan trips to Honduras. The purpose was to hand out water filters. I was not getting cooperation from anybody. The bishop in Honduras was way too busy to worry about what I was doing. I started to get discouraged. That afternoon, I looked at the situation. I did not come up with any answers. All of a sudden, a wind came into my apartment. It circled twice around my head. The Lord said, "I want you to do this."

Prostate Cancer

The miracle I experienced in my life was seven or eight years ago. I was showing signs of prostate cancer. Being a believer in Christ, I meditated on the word of God. I went through scriptures and fasted. When I went to the cancer doctor, he ran an ultrasound. He did more tests on me. No cancer was found. He did find a legion on my kidney. The doctor could not understand that. I gave all the glory to God.

Seven-Foot Angels

I remember about four years ago. I had just gotten off the bus. I had about five big bags of groceries. They were so heavy. I looked both ways to cross an intersection. There was not a person or car in sight.

I had set the groceries down. I picked up the bags and felt a tap on my shoulder. I looked around and saw a guy seven feet tall. He said, "I will carry the bags for you." He carried all the bags. He did not say much; he was very silent. So I got to my apartment and got five bucks out of my purse to pay him. He was gone. I asked my friend next door if she had ever seen a seven-foot-tall guy, with blonde hair. She said, "What are you talking about?" No person like that lives in this neighborhood. Especially a white guy. A week later, I went to the store again. I bought more than I could carry. Another guy that was seven feet tall helped me. He was different; he had brown hair. He was very quiet.

When I reached my door, the same thing happened. He disappeared. I told my friend about this. She said, "You just saw two angels. They helped when you were in need." I will never forget that!

Drown

A boy was under water, at least five maybe ten minutes. He has no brain damage and is doing fine. That is something only God could make happen.

Canal

I survived a car crash. I was speeding and lost control. I ran into a canal. Fortunately, it was not filled up. I would have drowned. It is a miracle that I survived.

Something Else

O n July 23, 2002, I was taking a friend home. We saw a Nisson Pathfinder flip seven times. We stopped and helped the guy and his family collect their belongings. There were suitcases open. He walked away. I thought that was a miracle. He was taking a lease car back to turn in. They were going from the United States to Germany. We gave them a ride.

His family was moving to Germany the next day. His wife and kids went to the doctor. We then took him to a hotel. His wife was a mental therapist. She helped returning soldiers with their mental health. I picked up my husband. We went to get something to eat. Coming back home, I saw a car pulling out of a Sonic. The car hit us in the right rear axle. Our vehicle flipped over and stopped upside down. I have some cut marks twelve years later. There are some issues in my left wrist. The accident was severe enough that they called a helicopter. I thought it was for a kid in the other car. It was for me. I was put on the helicopter.

Other than some stitches, I walked out of the hospital the next day. I feel like God was with me that day. I could feel angels all around me. I felt cloaked on all sides. I knew I would be all right. I felt a big hug from my deceased grandmother. I felt protected. It has stuck with me since. I celebrate every July 24. I know there is something else.

Not Homeless

I have been through a lot in my life. I dealt with drugs. I was homeless and lived on the street. Today, since I came to the knowledge of who Jesus Christ is, I do not get high. I am not homeless. No more living on the streets. Today, I am living for Jesus Christ. I am on fire for him. I thank God for who he is. I thank him for changing me from the inside out. I thank him for renewing my mind and giving me the mind of Christ. I thank him for cleaning me out and restoring me. I thank God for my family. I give him the glory, honor, and praise. If not for Jesus, I would be dead a long time ago. I want to thank him for cleaning me.

Ex Crack Addict

All glory to God. I am saved with the Holy Spirit today. I came from a life of crack cocaine and the lifestyle that went with it. Now, I am healed, healthy and blessed by my savior Jesus Christ. To God be the glory. I have found that Jesus is the savior. I was bound by sin in my mind. I was totally lost. Today, I am free, healed, healthy, and blessed. To God be the glory.

Depressed

I thank God for the salvation of my soul. I came from a background of depression. There was a tragedy in my life. It had a strong hold on me. I lost my will to do right or live. When I sought help, I was told there is something wrong with my brain. I would never be normal again. It is a lifelong problem. The Lord had a plan for me. I was delivered from my situation. I am so thankful that I am no longer depressed. I have a new life, full of love. I received more than I could ask for, abundantly, beyond all my expectations.

16-Year-Old Possessed

I was working in a juvenile intake office for the law. A sixteen-year-old female was brought in. She was on a hallucinatory drug. Coming down at that point, she had to be restrained because of her aggression. She was speaking in weird languages. She screamed and yelled. There was something in her possessing her. She threatened to kill us and herself. I was assigned to watch her. I prayed to God to take care of this girl.

She had too much to lose. She had a family. Most people in jail have nobody. They do not care. They feel they have nothing to lose. This little girl had a family waiting. Her mom and dad were waiting for her to straighten out. At the end of my prayer, she stopped talking to herself. Within seconds, she calmed down. She did not know I was there. I was off to the side. We had done everything we could to stop her. She got shots to put her to sleep. It got to a point where we fastened her down and waited for her to fall asleep. The meds were not doing anything. I just asked God to take care of this. I prayed for her safety. As soon as I got done with that prayer, she calmly looked at me. I then finished the intake processing. I thought that was a blessing.

Kidney

My son was born in 1978. He was in the hospital five days. He only weighed three pounds. It was a full-nine-month pregnancy. After five days, the hospital decided to keep for him ten days. I brought him home on the tenth day. The doctor said everything was fine. The day I brought him home, he started throwing up at about seven or eight in the evening. I had not had a baby in five years. I figured I diluted the milk wrong. I took him to a clinic. They said they needed to put him in the hospital. The Methodist hospital was across the street. I took him there to be admitted. They said, "Go home, everything will be fine. We will call you if anything goes wrong." I got home, and the phone was ringing. It was the hospital saying my son had to have an emergency surgery.

I said, "Go ahead and do what you have to do." I then went to the hospital to sign papers.

A doctor came out and told me, "Your son was born with a partial kidney. It is defective. It is not working. What we have to do is take off all that is defective. The little piece left will grow as the baby grows." He said it is a six-hour operation. He was in surgery for twenty-four hours. I figured he was dead, and they had not told me. I rushed in the room. My baby was all full of blood. There were about ten people around him. They escorted me out. The doctor said, "It took so long, because your baby died on the operating table." So I went and prayed.

I said, "Lord, let my baby live. If anything, take me instead." I had one request. "Before I go, let me lose some weight."

I was kind of big. To me that was kind of selfish, but that is what I wanted. They released my son. They said he would have to return at five. He had a hole in his heart. I prayed and prayed. I never did lose weight. When he was six years old, he had open heart surgery. Everything went fine. His kidney gave out when he was twenty-eight years old. He was put on kidney dialysis for three months. If we did not get a donor, he would die. One of my other sons donated a kidney. It worked fine. My son is now thirty-six and doing fine. That is a miracle.

Mustard Seed

A baby was born premature. It weighed one and one half pounds. Despite this small start, there are no complications. Everything is fine. Kind of reminds me of a mustard seed.

Sunflower

My father was in hospice. He slipped into a coma. Before doing that, he looked out the window. He said, "Look at the sunflowers." We looked out the window and didn't see anything.

We said, "Okay, Dad." We drove north to where my mother and his parents were buried. We were walking in the graveyard. My wife called me to look down a hill. There were sunflowers everywhere.

Four and a Half Months

Four and a half months ago, my mom passed away from breast cancer. My nephew, who was only twenty-three, died from leukemia ten months later. Now my brother-in-law needs a liver and kidney transplant. He has been in the hospital, in and out for over a year. We were told Friday that they have a perfect match coming from Oklahoma this afternoon. So he will get both organs.

Dialysis

A man had dialysis and five heart surgeries. He had tubes put in his arms. He passed away about two years ago. Before that, he went through some miracles. He had fallen into a near-death experience on a table for five or six hours.

Nonbeliever

I don't believe in God. I am a Catholic.

After talking to this homeless man for a while, he went to the library to listen to Bible audios. He could not read. He went from not believing to total belief in fifteen minutes.

Grace

There was an Easter pageant in World War Two. It was at a church. The pastor noticed that the congregation was almost all women. He asked where all the men were. They said at the bar. They thought that what they did in the war was something that made them not good enough for God. They felt they were not worthy of his grace. The pastor went over to the bar. He asked them why they felt they were not worthy of God's grace. They said they felt they had to work for it. The pastor said, "I have an Easter pageant that needs to be set up. It will tell the story of Jesus Christ. Let me put you guys to work." Half of the men turned to God. They realized his grace.

Psychic and Satanistic Ritual

My whole family is psychic. They are real spiritual, except for my brother. We have witnessed a bunch of things. My sister, when she was growing up, had a bad feeling about going to a birthday party. She was eighteen years old. She had a vision of her best friend holding up her child. There were a bunch of black, dark-looking creatures flying around her. She got hysterical. She got my mother to contact her friend's mother. She said her daughter was going to a birthday party. My sister said she went somewhere else. She is in danger. They found out where she was. She was at a satanistic ritual. They were going to sacrifice animals. She had no intention of getting involved with this. She got into it before she knew what was happening. Another thing, my sister went to visit my father in Sidney, Australia. She ended up getting in one of those cults. It was a huge cult, known all over the world.

It had been three and a half months past the time she was coming back. My mom was fearful. She did a lot of background checking on this group. They go after young impressionable people. My sister was wanting an answer from God, some type of sign. My mom called the day before she was to go to India with the group. Heroin was part of the deal. My mom got her and brought her home. One more day would have been too late. My sister had seen many visions in her life. She was too curious. One time she saw an airplane with people falling out. Seven years later, the same plane number of 777 crashed in the ocean.

Resuscitated

About three months after I became a Christian, a wild event took place. I was riding my bike to the supermarket. Coming back, I saw a big crowd in a parking lot. A crowd of people were looking at a person lying down. A young man about twenty-eight years old was being resuscitated. He was not breathing. He had red hair. His skin had turned blue-green. The man died.

He had a big tattoo of the angel of death. I wanted badly to tell the man about heaven. I did not know much about heaven. Something overwhelmed me from the inside. I started praying and crying. I was thinking about him waking up so I could tell him about Jesus. He opened his eyes after twenty-two minutes. His skin was turning pink. A happiness and joy overwhelmed me. Two minutes later, the ambulance arrived. I asked the driver where he was going. I went home and took a shower. After about one hour, I went to the hospital. I went inside the emergency room. There were a lot of nurses and beds. I asked about the person, "About two hours ago, a man died."

"Oh, the person who was dead. He is over there." I saw the man in a chair thinking deeply. I asked him if he knew me from the parking lot. I said, "Your skin was the skin of a dead person. I don't know the reason, but the Lord raised you up." He started crying. He told about going to the church as a young man. At sixteen, he rebelled.

He was divorced, addicted to drugs, and in trouble with the law. I said, "Listen, for some reason, God let you live. You were dead. I can testify to that." I plugged him into a church that believed in miracles. I had nothing to do with this. I was just there, and experienced the power of God.

Escalator

I was in the Air Force. I was stationed in Germany. My mom came to visit my wife and son. He was small at that time. At the airport, my wife put our son in a basket (stroller). She was going up an escalator. At first, everything was going smooth. Then she lost control of the stroller. Out of nowhere, a man put my son on the landing. She went to thank him, and he was gone.

Bar Fight

My dad is usually a very kind person. A guy at a bar picked a fight with him. The guy hit my dad. My dad looked at him and said, "What are you doing?" He hit my dad again. Finally, he hit back. A cop came in and only saw my dad hit back. He could not see well in jail that night. When he got out. He went to a doctor. They found a huge tumor that had been growing on his pituitary gland. It was starting to take over his vision. He had surgery, and took most of the tumor out. So far, everything has been good. The bar incident, probably, saved his life. He said he felt different after the surgery. He was overweight but started getting in shape. He started eating better. I am thankful that he is all right at the moment. It could have been worse.

Highway 35 and Flat Angel

Something happened several years ago. I had broken down on Highway 35 on my way to work. It was pouring down rain. At that time, the highway did not have very much of a shoulder to pull over on. It was very narrow. Because it was pouring down rain, I thought nobody would stop. Anyway, a man stopped and offered to help me. He put the spare tire on. The thing that made it a miracle was, the flat was on the same side as the traffic flow. The fact that anyone would risk their life to fix that tire was amazing. After he changed the tire, I tried to hand him a five-dollar bill. I noticed an aura around him. He was not wet, despite the rain still pouring down. He said no to the money. If my mother or sister were in this situation, I would want someone to help them too. I turned around, actually looked out of my window, and he was not there. I know that God sent me an angel that day. I have always considered it my angel miracle story. Definitely my guardian angel.

Leg and Hip Sciatica

I had major surgery five weeks ago for breast cancer. It was very long, about eight hours. Prior to the surgery, I had been in a lot of pain with something else. It was sciatica (a nerve disease) in my left leg and hip. I was worried about going into this surgery with this pain. I just gave it to God. I just said, "Lord, I am going to trust you." When I woke up from surgery, there were no signs of sciatica. No pain remained. God had completely healed me. I thank God for that miracle. I really needed that miracle. It helped me. Shortly afterward, another miracle happened. Three days later, I had a hematoma (a blood loss problem).

It could have killed me. I lost a lot of blood. I was still in the hospital. I had been scheduled for release earlier. Being there saved my life. I went into emergency surgery. I remember telling God, "I am not afraid of living or dying. But I really want to live." I feel like God is there at every turn.

Nothing

Everything we do in life is about God. It is not about anybody else. My miracles are about being left with nothing. I am still standing tall and stronger than I ever was before.

Helicopter

I have had divine intervention on two occasions. I was with a friend, and we were going to take a helicopter ride to Catalina Island from California. We were next in line. I had to go to the restroom. I thought, *I better go now because we are going on a helicopter ride.* So I tell my friend, "Let's let the people behind us go ahead of us." I went to the restroom. While I was there, I heard a big crash. When I came out, I was told the helicopter took off and turned upside down and crash-landed into the water. We were in shock. That should have been us. Thank goodness, the people were okay. That was definitely divine intervention. Another time, my mother had just passed. I celebrated on our birthdays. I always sing "Happy Birthday" to her. In addition, I always ask her to give me a sign of some sort. My best friend was visiting me. I kept repeating all day, "Mom give me some type of sign." It is my birthday, and I want to say hello. We went to Walmart at about two in the afternoon. Someone said on the intercom, "Angela, please come to the courtesy desk. Angela Ortiz, please come to the courtesy desk." Well, that was my mother's name. What chance would it be that that happened when we were in Walmart? For us to walk in and hear that was wild.

My best friend said, "There is your sign. She is saying hello." We hurried over to the courtesy desk to see who Angela Ortiz was. There was no Angela Ortiz. We asked the lady if they just called for Angela Ortiz. She said no. Very strange. My friend saw the whole thing. We were both in shock.

Model T

I went to El Paso one time. We broke down on the highway. I was talking to a guy that had broken down on the highway. A guy in a Model T pulled up and helped them out. When they looked up, the Model T was nowhere on the highway.

Chef

The following is a story of persistence, of never giving up.

I have grown in the last two years. I have had surgery twenty-seven times. I keep going, despite my physical limitations. I work, even though every indicator says I can't. I cook and deliver food to my family members. I take this unannounced. That is probably the most miraculous thing for me. I am studying to be a chef.

Prison Falling

The thing that happened in my life is working since my mother passed away in temporary and odd jobs. I have my own apartment, food, and furniture. My miracle is a pay raise and another job. Then my baby sister got hit by a car. The car was going about eighty miles per hour. It hit her whole body. It was torn up. I then got in trouble and went to prison. My sister came to see me in a wheelchair. Through the grace of God, she can now stand on her own. I fell from a two-story building and am fine now. These things happen when you believe in miracles.

Trust God

Trust God with all your heart and lean not on your own understanding. I was released from prison. I got an apartment. I was able to pay three month's rent. With no money, no job, and no prospects, I have made it. Jesus is more than you think.

Whooping Cough

I was a preemie in 1942, born in Santa Rosa downtown medical center. In those days, they did not have all the medical miracles they have today. The doctor told my mother and father that he could only save one of us. I was two months early. The nuns at the hospital took care of us. I got to come home on Christmas Day. My parents baptized me at that time. Six weeks later, I got the whooping cough. Again, the doctor told my parents that I wasn't going to make it. Well, here I am, seventy years later. That was a big miracle.

Four-Wheeler

I had a four-wheeler accident one night. I was going about forty-five miles per hour. I did not have a helmet on. The next thing I knew was I was upside down from the wreck. I didn't even have a scratch on me. I got up and tried to start the four-wheeler. It would not start. So I walked a couple miles home. I got my truck and retrieved the four-wheeler. I had a concussion, and that was it.

Hole in the Heart

A lady's daughter was born with a hole in her heart. She had congestive heart failure. The doctor said she would not make it. She is now a young lady with no problems.

Brakes

I was going to work about seventy miles per hour on the interstate. There was an accident in the right lane. I was in the middle lane. Suddenly, a car pulls from the right lane to the center in front of me. I braked and did not hit him. I do not know how. The car was so close, it was not normally possible to stop. There was no brake sliding noise. Nothing made sense. I felt like somebody was holding the car. It was not the brakes. I believe it was a miracle. It was special.

Hydroplane

It was raining very hard. I was about to enter the freeway. A car splashed in front of me. I started to hydroplane. My vehicle was not touching the ground, and I lost control. I thought my time had come. I spun around four times. I just missed entering the highway. I was fine, the car was fine. I felt God protected me.

Faith

A man went into a hamburger place. He fired his gun five times. All he got was five clicks. He went outside, and the gun fired shots. When he went back in, he attempted to shoot three times, Same result. The gun would not fire. He was not able to hurt anybody. He was arrested without incident.

Cancer Prayer

A man with liver cancer went to the hospital. He was told he had three months to live. He underwent chemotherapy. Through the power of God, he is mostly fine several years later. He has other issues though. He cannot walk without much back pain, and the man walks every day in the morning. He believes, "Be it so according to your faith."

A woman had cancer. The doctor was seen in a dream by her husband. It was before this happened. Dreams have meaning and not easy to interpret. She went to three doctors to see if she actually had cancer. She had cancer. After much prayer, the cancer was gone.

Car Flip

A twenty-six-year-old man had a serious car wreck. The car turned over. Amazingly, he did not even have a scratch.

Dog Home

A lady left town for a few days. Her friend watched her dog for her. The dog had never been at this place before. The lady came home from work, and the gate was open. The dog was gone. It had let itself out of the gate. It went to the owner's house.

EMT

I am in school to take a class and become an emergency medical technician (EMT). I was a little down in the dumps for a while. I was supposed to start the class in June, but I did not have the money at the time. It was a six-month course. I checked on the class when I got the money. It turned out that I registered on the last day that I could. That was lucky to me. Actually, it was meant to be. Because I wanted to learn how to save lives, I felt I was helped.

Eight Hours in Cold

I am a recovering drug addict. My mother ran a food pantry in a small town. It was called Helping Hands Food Factory. Throughout my addiction, I worked at the food pantry. I gave my life to the Lord. I believed in God and believed that Jesus saved me. I felt I would be used, no matter where I was. When I was addicted, I went to court in the snow. I drove past a car on the side of the road. I was thinking people on their cell phone were calling a wrecker. So I went to court, and things did not turn out the way I would have liked. I ended up going back about one o'clock in the morning. Something told me to look where that car was.

The people were still in the car. So I pulled over to the side of the road. These people had been in the car with no heater for eight hours. The motor had blown. They could not speak English, and I could not speak Spanish. So. I called my Spanish girlfriend. She translated for us. I had no driver's license or insurance. I was concerned about being on the side of the road, helping these people. A highway patrol pulled up. Instead of taking me to jail, he knew I was doing the right thing.

I drove these people about three hundred miles back home. I knew that that was what I was put there to do. I believe that in what you are doing, if the Lord has put his hand on you, he is going to use you in any condition you are in. He forgave you. As long as you are doing the things he wants you to do, he looks past your shortcomings. You were born a sinner.

You take a six-month-old kid and an eighteen-month-old kid. The younger kid has a bottle, and the older kid takes it and starts to drink it. Momma then steps in and retrieves the bottle. That eighteen-month-old was not taught to steal. It came naturally. The miracle is, after twenty-five years of addiction, the Lord has taken the need of getting high away.

I was in the penitentiary. Every time the parole review came up, I was refused. Until I honestly turned my ways over to the Lord, to be used in the way I needed to be used, I would not be free in any way. I surrendered my will to him. He did what I asked him to. He will not lead me anywhere that is wrong. The temptations are not going to tempt me anymore. I gave it all to him; my life is his. For an active meth addict, that is a miracle.

Atheist

I met a guy in New Mexico. I had been locked up. Now, I was doing a Bible study. I was also doing another Bible study in California. An atheist came into a Bible study. He was treated really bad because of his commentary. I stopped the people from taking his stuff. I got to talking to him about the bible. Why did he not believe? He said his stepfather molested him as a child. He had not told this to anyone. He always thought it was something he did. He never had the feeling that God cared for him. I told him, "Every act of kindness in your life is an act of God. Human nature is to be greedy and selfish and dominate." I was sharing what I had with him.

He started going to church with me. He turned his life over to God. That is a miracle. God put me with this man to be a testimony of his love. He has never forsaken me. When you are put in a position to minister to somebody with so much hurt, you give them a part of yourself and make them a better person. That gives you a sense of fulfillment. That is part of your cup that is being full. The little trials become insignificant when the joy of the Lord becomes part of you.

Salvation Army Truck

I was on the Salvation Army truck, picking up donations. We pulled up to a house. There was a police motorcycle in the garage. The guy I was picking up from is a cop. He asked what we are about at the Salvation Army. I told him, "I am in the drug and alcohol rehabilitation center. We help people recover." He asked if I minded what I am in there for. I said, "No, I am in there for methamphetamines. I was a meth cook."

He looked at me and said, "My brother was a meth addict while I was in the army. He was in an accident and got hooked on this." He said he was so wrapped up in his army career, that he could not come to straighten this out. He said he would have beat it out of him to the point he would not use again. You could tell this man had a lot of pain and anguish in his life. He let it hang on his shoulder. He felt his brother being a drug addict was his fault.

I told him, "You do not understand drug addicts. They are not weak. It does not matter how many times you beat them. They will go back to what they are doing. There is nothing anybody can do or say to stop them. They have to decide to stop." After I talked to this man, you could see the tears running down his face. I was put there to release the burden that he was taking upon himself, all because of his brother's actions. The Lord put me on that truck, put me in this house, and put the words in my mouth to minister to this person to say the right things, not to just pick up the donations and leave. When he gets ready to use you, he is going to use you. If he can use me, he can use anybody.

Truck Tire

One day, I was working in a tire shop on an inverted machine. It had an angle facing you. Then a 16.5 tire blew up. It hit me in the chest and face area. It blew me about seven feet up and fifteen feet back. Instead of being killed, I only had a busted nose. I just threw the tire off me. My dad said, "If you ever do that again, I am going to kill you." About three days later, I made up a large truck tire. I just got through taking the air gauge off it. At that point, I was weary of tires. I backed away. It blew up and put a large dent in a truck. That was the last truck tire I fixed.

Dead Husband

I met my husband in 2001. He became my knight in shining armor. Seven years later, a lady ran a stop sign and ran over him. He lasted four hours and seventeen minutes. At the hospital where he passed away, the doctor asked if I wanted to donate his organs. My husband was a kind man with a big heart. I did not know what to do. So I called his brother. He said the driver was driving like a maniac, and he said yes about donating his organs. I gave his corneas away and also his heart valve. He gave sight to two people in south Texas, and he helped a man repair his heart. My miracle is when he was killed, my parishioner helped us get a traffic light at the accident scene. This was a very dangerous spot. There had been four or five accidents a week there. There was just a stop sign. Every day I pass, I am thankful for the traffic light. No doubt it saves many lives. Our community is now safer. That is a miracle in my life.

Lightning

A man was struck by lightning on the head. Fire then came out of his fingertips. But he said he did not feel any bad effects from the incident. He is fine today.

Cougar

I just want to thank the Lord. My daughter got mauled by a cougar. That happened when she was two years old. She is now thirty-three years old. She is doing well now.

Climb Out of the Hole

I am not exactly sure if this counts as a miracle. But it is close. I used to have a friend named Joe. He had a terrible life. He was abandoned by his dad, and his mother raised him. He got into drugs, weed, and other harder things. I met him at the skating ring, and we started skating together. Then I got involved with weed.

We used to talk every night. One time, he told me he felt like he was in a hole. He had been in alterative for a long time. He was out now. He said he could not get out of the hole. He didn't know how to climb anymore. He asked me what to do. At that time, I really didn't know what to say. But I tried of course. I was his friend. I read him a story that I had been working on at that time.

We had a large group of friends that would skate. We would all hang out every day. We were just a bunch of delinquent little kids. Joe had the hardest case. He had the raw end of the deal all the time. I told him, "There are great things in this world. They will not come immediately or even the way you want them to be. I started reading after I got sick of my lifestyle at the time." He just looked at me.

He asked how I could be so optimistic. "There are such terrible things in the world."

I told him, "I don't know. I still don't know why I am optimistic." After that night, he quit smoking. He went to college. And he is climbing!

Premature

A girl was born one week premature. She was in serious condition. Now, she is eight years old, and she is the biggest person in her class.

Median Grandma

A guy was going down a road. It was the normal route he took from work to home. He then went down a different road one day. He did not know why. He saw a car on the median. It was not wrecked. As he wondered, *What is anyone doing up there?* he realized it was his grandmother. He turned back around and helped. There was a reason for that. There is a reason for everything.

Cut Open

In 2001, I went to have cancer surgery. Seven tests said I had pancreatic cancer. I had so many churches praying for me. My entire family also prayed. I went in to surgery. After cutting me open, there were no signs of cancer. I had internal ultrasounds, external ultrasounds, and a colonoscopy. Everything you could imagine. I was told, "You have pancreatic cancer and will probably die."

Deathly Ill

I was in high school. In my senior year, I got deathly ill. It was in February. I was close to death. I was sick for about three months. I had lost about forty pounds. The doctors did a lot of tests on me. I talked to some people in my church. They came in and gave me a blessing. After about one week, I rapidly healed. I had not had any drugs or artificial help. I was preparing to play college sports. My life was spared, and I am now totally healthy. That is my miracle.

D

In North Branch, Iowa, we had the sesquicentennial. It was the 150th year anniversary. I worked on a committee of eight people. We were deciding what to write. This book took one year to finish, edit, and print, and the book took first place in the state of Iowa. Finally, we were entered in a national contest. We went to Portland, Oregon. We took first in our category. I thought that was quite an accomplishment. In school, my grade in English and literature was D.

Vegas Last Hoorah

I was in college in Texas. My roommate was from Iowa. I asked how he ended up there from Iowa. He said he read that that was the most partying place to go. I laughed. We were very good friends, and he had other friends from Iowa at the college. We saw each other after graduation about once a year. We had families and little spare time. You know, "How are you doing?" then catch up on the last year of life. Well, after we got much older, he called and said he was dying of cancer. He said he was going to Las Vegas with his friends. I said, "Count me in." We all met in Las Vegas for his last hoorah. He seemed fine. We had a lot of fun for several days. On the last day, he was so tired we had to get a wheelchair. We all went back home. He died four days later. When people know they are going to die, they typically get their loved ones and friends together one last time. He knew that this was it. Nothing is stronger than love. It was a miracle that we all got together one last time.

Two-Hundred-Mile Mother

My dad and I have lived together about four years. I lost my job and moved two hundred miles away. I stayed with my mother, till I got a job. This was before I got married. I was going to tell my girlfriend to either come live with me, or we are done, an ultimatum so to speak. I knew she would not leave. She had two kids. Well, she got pregnant a week after I moved. We had tried to have a baby for a year. Then when I didn't want to, she got pregnant. I moved back, and we got married. Our baby is now two years old. She is healthy as can be.

Pregnancy Cancer

I was extremely abused as a child. I did not know exactly how bad it was until I became an adult. In the last year, I have lost my mother, grandmother, and both of my children. The children did not die but were taken from me by child protective services. I learned to find who I am inside. I became an overcomer. No matter what happened, I moved forward. God gives me the power to see the positive in everything each new day. My oldest daughter is battling cancer. She is eighteen years old. We caught it just in time when she had gotten pregnant. When she was checked, the cancer was revealed. If not for the pregnancy, we would have never known she had cancer.

TV Shrapnel

I went to Iraq in 2004. We had a military convoy. We slept a few hours, then stopped to eat. On the way back, I got a television. We received artillery fire. It injured my arm and leg. The television saved my life. If I did not have it, my vital area would have been shot. The television took a lot of shrapnel. It definitely took the brunt of the blow. I was so glad I got that television. Another marine with me got shot all over his body. Of course he died. I have had seventy-three surgeries in my lifetime.

Endometriosis

When I was eighteen, I was diagnosed with endometriosis. At twenty-three, I had two surgeries. The second one, they went in and burned my uterus completely out. I was told I would never have kids again. Within one year, I was pregnant. I had a lot of complications during the pregnancy, and my daughter was born not breathing. They rushed her to the nursery. They put her on oxygen. After that, she was perfectly fine and healthy. She is a blessing.

Look-Alike Dad

When I was living in Nevada with my aunt and uncle, I was seventeen. We went on a little picnic together with my grandma, together my aunt, my uncle, and their two little girls. We were having a nice, quiet little picnic in a remote beautiful park. While we were sitting there and talking, a couple suddenly appeared on a table next to us. They were very quant. They had little lanterns on top of their table. Angelic is how they appeared. When the man turned and looked at us, my grandma almost fainted. He looked exactly like my deceased dad. I wanted to cry. It had been about twelve years since he passed. We were all devastated, because he looked so similar.

He was identical. His eyes were a beautiful blue. He was tall, like my dad. He spoke very softly. He came over to our table and asked how we were doing. He also asked where we're from. He mentioned how beautiful the park was. Basically, he kept very small conversation. He concentrated mainly at me. He looked directly at me as he talked. He asked how I was doing and if I was happy. I thought that was strange for a stranger to ask me that. But I felt very comfortable talking with him. He looked so much like my dad.

When we were leaving, he was standing by a big tree. The headlights were facing him. His lady friend was very quiet. She said very little. As he looked at us, he put his right hand to his heart and waved bye with his left hand. When my father passed away in the hospital, he put his right hand over his heart and waved good-bye with his left hand. It was a chilling experience. To this day, we think that was him. They told us where they were from. It did not exist when we looked at a map.

Little things were mentioned that did not make sense to us. We know it was a miracle.

Disappearing Man

A guy and his girlfriend were on a road in the country. There was nobody around. All of a sudden, they saw a man with a beard in front of them. As they got closer to investigate, he disappeared.

Divorced Dad

There was an incident when I was young, about six years old. My parents had a really bad divorce. My dad was really mean to my sister and me after the divorce. When I lived with my dad, it was really bad. It was so bad, eventually I left his house. I could not be with him anymore. This happened twice. Both times, I did not see him for about a year. One day, my sister said he had called. He wanted to see us again. I was really scared about it. The first moment I talked to him, my heart opened up. I forgave him for all he had done. Now, we have a good relationship. He still has problems with the divorce. Everything is not good with him. We actually love him now and enjoy spending as much time as we possibly can.

Severed Glass

I was in a car accident when I was about six or seven years old. It was a serious accident. My mom and I went straight into a tree. The windshield shattered, and the glass cut my entire face. My upper lip was completely severed off. I had to get plastic surgery for my upper lip. It was a *miracle* that I was alive. Glass was flying everywhere. It could have easily severed my throat.

No Brain Damage

My son and I were in a real bad accident when he was five years old. I had stepped away from the church. The doctor said he probably would not make it. He was thrown from the car. He was in the trauma center. My mom is a very faithful person. She was walking around the hospital with a little prayer card. She told me, "Your son is going to be fine." (It reminds me of Jesus talking to the centurion.) The doctor said he was in a coma. If he came out, the doctor said he would have brain damage. I told my husband that my mom had gone crazy. "How does she know my son will wake up?" The next morning, the nurses said they have good news. My son woke up. The brain damage was still a question. He recognized us immediately. He recognized all of us. It restored my faith. It was a miracle. He survived with no brain damage.

Job Transfers

After the death of my son, my family was located in Colorado Springs. My son was killed in Iraq. It became a bit overwhelming there. Sometime after that, we came to San Antonio to a place we were familiar with. I had great childhood memories of San Antonio. We decided this is where we needed to be. My husband and I went back to Colorado. We looked for jobs in the San Antonio area. I remember so clearly how we got on our knees and prayed. We held hands and hoped for an opportunity to get new jobs. We wanted to start fresh. My husband was not a real religious man, but he believed in God. He held my hand, and we prayed for these jobs. The next day, my husband got called for a job interview. Unfortunately, he did not get the position. That did not keep us from continuing to take a leap of faith. Approximately three months later, my husband received a notification for a job.

We still lived in Colorado Springs. He e-mailed me the requisition. I looked at it. It was an awesome opportunity. The pay was more. It would be a promotion to a position two steps higher. It involved more responsibility, but it was the perfect position. I reminded him that we had to be together. There was not going to be two households. "He was here, I was there" setup would not work. We had to be together as a family. So I said to him, "That is awesome. It is too bad, so sad." I went back into a meeting. After about an hour and forty-five minutes, I received another e-mail. It looked very similar to the one my husband received. I thought, *Why on earth is he sending me this e-mail?* As I looked closer, I realized the job was actually for me. I called my husband and said, "This is incredible and unbelievable."

We decided when we got home, we would review the documents and talk about it. Not only were the job offers at the same time, but my husband's position included all moving expenses. They also bought the house. We were packed out by the new company. Here we are, four years later. This is a happy place. There is not too much grief overshadowing the good times we have had. We have been able to start over. We have a great life. We give all the glory to God. There is no other explanation as to how all this could have happened. It was simply the hand of God.

Uppers, Downers

I remember a time in my life when I was completely into drugs. Alcohol was also big in my life. I was in the party scene. It had been going on for a long time. One night, I decided to mix a bunch of drugs—uppers, downers, and acid. I remember puking my guts out. I felt like I would die. I wrote a farewell note to Mom. I locked myself in the restroom, and I was able to throw up everything. I am so glad to be alive today. I was a survivor. Not many who were like me did that.

Mosquito Bite

A lady got bit by a mosquito when she was six years old. She contracted a virus. It was spread from cattle.

She was told she would not live by the doctor to the age of ten. She did live life in a wheelchair. She is now in her sixties. Her outlook on life is very good, and she is a happy person.

Library

I moved to a lake to be with my sister. Shortly afterward, she got sick. I helped her in all ways. It turned out that I became director of the library. It was one of the most beautiful buildings you will ever see. The library is a miracle. One thing leads to another.

Hospital Heart Attack

An elderly man was sitting at home. His heart was beating fast for four hours. He decided to go to the hospital. About thirty minutes after going to the hospital, he had a heart attack. He would have died if he were not in the hospital. He is doing fine now, but he does need to be careful. The fact he is alive and walking is a miracle. He is now running a restaurant. All of this happened for a reason.

Either Or

My youngest daughter was Tracy. She was my last child. I had a very rare condition when she was born—wherein 99 percent of the time, either the mother or child survived or they both do not survive. I was in the hospital for about seven and a half months. The doctors kept thinking I lost my child. The sonogram said she was still there. At the end of the pregnancy, I was told she had to be two and a half pounds to do a C-section. I was not okay either. They said she is not two and a half pounds. I said, "She was at least four pounds."

Another sonogram revealed she was big enough. The doctor spoke to my husband, who is an air traffic controller. He came from the control tower after another sonogram. We were told this was necessary before the surgery. He had to sign a paper stating whom he wanted to save. They do pump blood; however, the chance of survival was 1 percent for me to make it. So he chose to save the child. They did one last sonogram to see where she was positioned. The doctor said something was not right.

The head doctor came into the room. Only in an emergency would the head doctor inspect. He looked at the pictures. They said, "Well, I don't know. You can get dressed and go home."

I said, "Where is my baby?" The baby was fine. I was hooked up to machines and tubes. My husband was not back from work.

The doctor said the condition was gone. "You are fine. There is nothing wrong with you. You are perfectly okay."

I said, "All right." I put on my clothes and waited in the waiting room. My husband came in.

He asked, "What happened?"

I said, "It's gone."

He said, "What is gone?"

"The doctor said they did not know where it went."

He asked, "What is with this higher power?"

I said, "It is called God."

That is my story. My daughter is a beautiful nineteen-year-old now!

Turkish Dingy

I was stationed in Turkey in the army. It was 2001, and I was getting ready to leave. I had one week left before returning to the States. We were out on a boat; actually, it was a pontoon. We were having a party on the lake. Of course, as usual with folks in the military, there was some drinking involved. At one point, we stopped the boat. We all went swimming. After everyone was in the boat, we took off again. At a later point in time, somebody lost a slipper in the water. So me being me, I jumped in the water to get the slipper. For whatever reason, the guy driving the boat did not know I had jumped out. The boat just kept going. I started cramping up.

Not being able to swim anymore, I went under water. Some of the guys in the boat jumped in the water. One was a guy that worked for me. Me being a big guy was a struggle for this small man. It was such a struggle; he passed me off to somebody else. There was a lot of chaos going on. In the midst of this, they dropped me again. I went down again, and all he saw was my arms hanging up. He caught a glimpse of my watch. He grabbed me and dragged me back up again. They were struggling to get me up.

Out of nowhere, a Turkish fisherman appeared in a dingy. He saw what was going on. He grabbed me and put me on the boat. He looked like he weighed 100 pounds soaking wet. I am about 250 pounds. He grabbed me from his boat and threw me in our boat. How he had that much strength is a mystery. They did CPR on me. I was black and blue and purple. One of the customary things with the

Turks was paying money for their services. They are all about money. The guys were getting money together. They were going to pay him for helping us. When they turned around, he was gone. Nobody ever saw him again.

Premonition

This is a story of a premonition. My mother had a dream when she was about ten years old. She woke up screaming and crying. She dreamed a friend of ours, about three at the time, had gotten hurt. She was in the hospital holding the little girl while the doctors were working on her. The little girl was unconscious; however, my mother still told her everything would be okay. Waking up, she tried to get the girl's parents on the phone. By noon, we got a hold of them. We were told that she had grabbed an electrical fence. It electrocuted her really good. She was found unconscious. She had to be rushed in an ambulance. She was close to death. My mom did not know what was wrong. She did feel something terribly wrong. She had no idea what was going on. To this day, she said it is the most vivid dream she ever had.

Choking Brother

A man went into a bathroom at a restaurant. He started choking in a very serious way. Another guy came in behind him and performed the Heimlich maneuver. It saved his life. The guy that saved him said he did not have time to think. He just did what he did to help the guy. The man choking was Hispanic. The guy that saved him was black. The black man felt the Hispanic guy did not like black people. He was thanked in a major way by the wife. Now, it is a different story. We are all brothers.

Go With Flow

I go to college at Texas A&M. My original plan was to be an engineer. I was all set and had all the courses. I had the background in math that was needed. When it came to pursuing my engineering career, I ended up failing my classes. I was completely devastated. I did not know what I wanted to do with my life. I spoke to a counselor. They brought me to my new course—construction science. I am extremely happy where I am right now. I feel like I am in a good spot in my life. It made me realize that your dreams are not necessarily suitable for you until you test it. It happened for a reason. There is a reason for everything. The miracle is that I learned to go with the flow.

Second Cousin

The two following stories are about what appeared to be coincidence against all odds, but there are no coincidences.

My story starts with my next-door neighbor. Growing up, he was a football star at a junior college. His roommate would visit me quite often. During the four years in college, we became very close. He would even have dinner with my family. We hung out. He asked if we could take him to New Jersey. He wanted to see a cousin he had never met. We said sure. So he rode with us to New Jersey. We got to his cousin's house and let him out. He asked where we were going. We said we were going to see this woman that lived nearby. He goes, "Really! I have friends over there." We told him the woman's name. He asked, "Why are you going to see her?"

My mom said, "What do you mean?"

He said, "That is my cousin."

I said, "She can't be your cousin. She is my cousin." It turned out that his cousin was my second cousin. All the time in college, I had no idea that we were related.

Sam

This has to do with my family. My grandmother told this story about my oldest brother. His name was Sam. When he was young, he and my grandmother were very close. He left to make his own way in the world. We are a mixed race family. Sam had very light complexion. So he blended well with everyone. He was very passive. After he left, the family never saw or heard from him again. My grandmother never forgot him. She always told me, I reminded her of him. One year, my uncle went to New York. He was attending a funeral of another relative. After departing the train, he took a bus to the funeral home. Sitting on the bus, a man sat down next to him. They started talking. Through the conversation, they both find out they are going to the same funeral. My uncle asked why he was going to the funeral. "What is your relationship?" As the conversation went on, it turned out the man was Sam. He passed away a few weeks later. My uncle was the last person in the family to see Sam.

Costa Rica

This occurred on a train from San Jose, Costa Rica, to Baton. I was sitting there talking to a gentleman. I was telling him where I was going. The man in the seat in front of me overheard the conversation. He got up and said come with me. I had never seen this guy before. He said, "I have a place for you" twice.

I said, "I cannot go with you. I am new here and just arrived from traveling." It turned out he saved a seat for me in another car. He had gone up to a lady there and made sure she would take care of me. He asked her to buy any of the foods along the way. It was my first time in Costa Rica. Everybody spoke Spanish. He also secured a seat for me next to a window. I am a photographer. This was so I could take photographs. I offered to buy something to eat or drink. He would not accept. He walked off the train, and I never saw him again.

Barbed Wire

There was a hunting accident I was a part of. I was riding in the back of a truck. We were out night hunting for hogs. The driver of the truck hit a quarry of hogs. We lost control and I went through a barbed wire fence. The momentum from the collision knocked me out of the truck. All I remember was looking at my hand. I was out cold. I woke up in and out of conversations. I heard we have got to cut him loose. Also, to go get my pliers. What had happened was after being thrown out of the truck, I was wrapped up in a barbed wire fence. It was pretty close to a T post. I had a gash in my skull to the bone and two ribs broken next to my spine. It had to be popped back out. By the grace of God, I survived. They were trying to move the truck to get the lights on me. They did not realize that the wire was wrapped around the axle. I was being drug with the truck. They stopped and cut me loose. Then turned the truck around. It was scary how close I was to the rebar. Looking at me now, you would never know. I have no visible scars.

104.7

There have been so many times that I almost lost my life. One happened when I was pregnant. My child was stillborn. I went into the emergency room with a 104.7-degree temperature. The doctors were skeptical that I would survive. My parents were great believers in God. They prayed, and I survived. The baby was named Angel. I believe it has helped me through life. It was very difficult to lose my first child. I prayed a lot. Through my life, I have been very sick with respiratory illnesses. I have severe asthma. I cannot breathe at times. Sometimes, I was alone. I asked God to help me. I was being taken to a hospital a couple of years ago. I had a major attack.

I thought it would be my last breath. I asked God to help me because I could not breathe. After praying, I got a gush of air. A calmness came over me. I made it to the emergency room. I made it through that.

Dying With God

There are so many times after that. A couple of years ago, I had a kidney stone that was serious. I was very sick and confused. I did not answer the phone anymore. I just prayed for God to help me. A friend was trying to get me. She came to the house very concerned. She knocked with no response. She then called the police. Before the police got there, I finally heard the knocking. I was able to make it to the door. I opened the door and was taken to the hospital. I was very sick. The doctors said I was full of infection. I had a stint put in. After that, I was on an IV. They could not remove the stone until the infection was gone. It was very painful. I finally got the stone removed. I live alone and know God has helped me. There is no one else to help me. When I struggle with these illnesses, he is there. I don't feel like I will die alone, because he is always with me.

Cancer Gone

A friend of my mom's mother had cancer. The day before the surgery, they did one last scan. We had been praying for her. There was nothing there. The cancer was completely gone. The doctors could not understand. There was no medical explanation. There is a divine explanation. It is called the power of God.

$20

My mother and three kids were in a parking lot. An old lady with a shopping cart approached us. She appeared to be homeless. She asked my mom for five dollars to take a bus. She said she just needed that much more for the bus fare. My mom gave her last five dollars. My two siblings did not see the lady. They asked who mom was talking to. I saw and heard her clearly. The lady said thank you. She also told my mom she would be blessed four times over what she gave. At that point, she disappeared. After getting home, my dad asked my mom for money to eat. She said she gave her last five dollars to the lady. She looked in her purse. To her surprise, there was a neatly folded twenty-dollar bill.

Degree Recovery

A little girl was four years old. She had a fever of 105 degrees. Very near death, she went to the hospital.

As she was clinging to life, she said an amazing thing. Jesus was holding her on his lap. She recovered and is now seven years old. She no longer remembers what she said. Her parents and grandparents will never forget it. She was on the brink of death. A full recovery happened almost instantly. Incidents like these are undeniable. Jesus is real.

Alarm Code

Our home came with a security alarm system. We did not receive the four-digit code. Everything was fine. Then one day, the alarm went off. My wife turned it off with the four-digit code that came to her. Nobody told her what it was. The odds against figuring that are extremely high. It was a ten-digit keyboard. At least a million to one. The amount of different codes is huge. It was not a coincidence as there are none.

Shotgun

The miracle that happened to me was about five years ago. I was not hanging around a good crowd. I went to a friend's house to a party. A couple of guys down the street did not like my friend. We did not know they were planning on doing something. About one hour into the party, we got word that some people outside wanted to fight. I stayed in. A couple of guys went out there. After a fight, they came back in. My friend went outside. He was shot in the face with a shotgun (buckshot). There were pellets everywhere on his body. I could not even recognize him.

I was sitting down next to him. He got up and opened the door. It was only two feet away. All you could see was smoke—from under the door, both sides of the door, and from over his body. I could not think about anything. Nor could I hear anything. I turned to look at my friend. He was stumbling. While he was doing that, he was holding his face. Pretty much holding his jaw together. If he did not do that, his jaw would literally come off. The only thing that stopped me from going out was a voice telling me to sit down. Something told me, "Don't move." It saved me from being shot. My other friends in the house ran out and started firing.

Remember, this was a bad crowd. Two of them are in jail. My other friend that got shot almost passed away that night. He managed to survive. He is now working hard with a family now. He has a little girl. I could not be happier for him. Just to make it out alive, that is my miracle.

Five Years

I was told by doctors that my daughter would not survive after five years. She is now eleven years old. She is doing fine.

Sickle Cell

The miracle I experienced was with my late sister. She was born February 11, 1970. Two weeks later, she was diagnosed with sickle cell anemia and cerebral palsy. The doctor said she would not live to be eleven years old. But my parents and I believe that through God and faith, she lived to be thirty-one years old. My sister could not walk. She could talk and think fine. My parents and I provided a normal environment. We treated her like she didn't have any disability or handicap. She was very independent. She went to public school and graduated high school in 1989.

I had the privilege of escorting her across the stage to get her high school diploma. She worked as a greeter for a theme park. While doing that, she went to college. She travelled a lot. She went to Hawaii in 1989 with my mother. She was active in sports. She was the first to water ski for handicapped people in the theme park. Also, she met famous people—David Robinson and his parents and different groups in music. She was well travelled. She was part of the youth department at Mount Sinai Baptist church. She died on April 22, 2001. She was thirty-one. She accomplished things most healthy people never do. That includes myself. She was a very loved person.

Cloud Cross

My mother was diagnosed with stage 4 colon cancer. She died in September 2008. She had never gone to church, but she was a spiritual woman in her own way. When she passed away, I walked outside. I was really shocked at the time. I had walked outside from her townhome. It was a crisp evening in the fall. I looked up to the sky and asked God for a sign. I needed to know she was okay. The clouds formed a cross. There was someone at the foot of the cross. I will never forget it. I had my sister come outside. She looked up and saw the same thing.

Sixty-Nine-Year-Old

I was born on February 6, 1948. The day I was born, the doctors told my parents that I would not live to be ten. I was born a blue baby. I am now sixty-nine years old.

Motorcycle Accident

In 1968, I had a motorcycle. A lady ran a stop sign. I hit her car broadside at seventy miles per hour. I was not wearing a helmet. I messed up my left hand and my right leg. I spent some time in the hospital. It is a wonder I didn't die from that accident.

Jack Stand

On April 11, 2012, I had a ten-thousand-pound vehicle fall off a jack stand. It fell on top of me. I remember very well, saying, "Oh God, please don't let me die now. I am not done with what I want to do." For some reason, God saved me. That totally destroyed me. They took out my left kidney. I bruised my heart and partially collapsed my lungs. I bruised my colon and liver. I broke my kidney in two. I had my left kidney removed. But I am still here. I believe it is the grace of God—a miracle for me. Now, I am trying to find my purpose. Why am I still living, what does he want me to do? What can I do for him, to serve him for what he has done for me? That is my question.

Walker at Two

My daughter had a rare disorder. She is now five. Low muscle tone was a main symptom. If I picked her up, she was like a ragdoll. She would just flop. She could not cry or do anything. The doctor said they did not know what was wrong with her. He said we would have to learn to live with it. We finally found a neurologist who figured it all out. The doctor said she would not be able to walk until she was five. She actually started walking at two. We had gotten a wheelchair for her, based on what we were told. The doctors were astounded. They were amazed at her rapid progress.

Guardian Angels

My mom told me about a bad car accident when I was little. My dad hit a car. We flipped about eight times. I was three and my sister was two. She flew out of the window and landed underneath a vine. I only had a few cuts. I told my mom that I saw two men in white. They pulled us out of the car. I don't remember the accident. Apparently, we were saved by guardian angels.

Bad Choices

I was born and raised in church. I thought I was saved, but I really was not. I was just going through the motions. I was not making good decisions as far as guys in my life. I was in some really bad relationships. My sons were not that great. I was always very permissive with the men in my life. When I met a guy, I thought I was in love for the first time. He did and said all the right things. After having sex, a realized a few days later that it was not love. It was lust. I was really broken. It drove me into a really bad depression where I wanted to commit suicide. I was cutting myself. I tried to fill a void that could only be filled by God. I kept going in a downward spiral. After a couple months, I went to church and gave it all to God. I gave all the broken pieces so I could be made a masterpiece. My biggest miracle is God picked me up when I was very down. The void and depression were healed. Now I am living for God. I could not be happier.

Duffel Bag

I was living in Belgium. I had a large duffel bag. It was really heavy. I had it at the house, and my dad visited. He tossed it in the cellar. A couple of hours later, the bag had been dragged across the floor. Every time we put something there, it would move. We were talking to our landlord. He informed us our house was built on a battleground. There was no explanation for what occurred.

Under Bridge

I was talking to a lady at the food store. She was telling me she met a Hispanic man under the bridge. She and her husband brought him home and fed him. They noticed he seemed kind of wacky. They were not sure what was going on. She asked if she could place some oil in the palm of his hand. He was kind of freaking out but said, "Go ahead, whatever." She did that and started praying to him and for him. A miracle happened, and he is no longer on heroin. He is an amazing person, very grateful. He actually followed her around for a whole hour. He asked, "What did she do?" He could tell something miraculous had happened, and he never went back to drugs. Praise God.

Flat to School

My son was a college student. He goes to work at the same time every day. He was heading off to school and had a flat tire. He changed the tire. He found out that the delay saved him from an accident at the entrance to school. It happened at the exact time he is at that point. That flat tire saved him, and the person that got hit was killed.

Run Over Twice

A man got run over; then, another vehicle ran over him. He should not have been here. Nobody but God could save him. His healing was a slow, steady progress. He now has two kids. From having a broken body, he learned to walk again. He went from a wheelchair, to a cane, to no help.

Blown-Up Truck

A partner of mine drove an eighteen-wheeler. He was involved in a head-on collision. The other guy had been drinking all night. My friend was able to kick himself out when the vehicle turned over. He got out of the truck, and the truck blew up. When he woke up, he was at the hospital and did not know how he got to the hospital.

Twenty-Two Accident

When I was twenty-two, I was involved in a really bad car accident. I did not have my seatbelt on. The car was hit by two different vehicles. The front seat and backseat were gone. I was thrown into the one part of the car that did not get crunched. I broke a nail, and that was it. The rest of the car was destroyed. My son was not in the car that day. That was very unusual. He was supposed to be. That was the miraculous thing that happened in my life.

Mask

I just got back from another town. I was on the esplanade one day. I took a nap and was out there for a long time. When I woke up, there was a huge whiteout going on. No water was available. It was about a four-hour walk from town. I had asthma and needed a mask bad. Just when I thought I could not go any further, I saw a piece of trash blow by. I picked up the bag. Inside was a wrapped-up face mask and goggles. They were brand new. The weird part is they came out of nowhere. I put them on and made it home.

Swimming Pool

I was at a public swimming pool when I was five years old. My sisters and I were playing catch. I jumped up to catch the ball and landed in the deep end of the pool. I literally saw kids swimming on the surface of the water. And I saw Jesus on the water. I was afraid and scared. The next thing I knew was a hand pulled me up. I was rescued and didn't drown.

Health Issues

I have had numerous health issues. I almost died at birth. I have had many seizures. The many health issues I have survived cannot be explained. I do not know how I am alive. I was born premature with a slight chance to live. I have been beating the odds to this day.

Church Parking Lot

I took a turn and blew out both front tires. I lost control and was on two tires. I ended up in a church parking lot. I was in between a kiosk (sign) and a telephone pole. On the kiosk, it said "God Saves All." About six months after that, I was playing around coming off the interstate. I crashed my truck again. The funny part is I had popped a tire and tried to get the truck off the street before a police officer showed up. So I pulled into a house real quick. The lady at the house was extremely nice. Her husband pulled up in a car. He was a pastor. You might say God was trying to get my attention.

Bone Marrow

My mom was diagnosed with a bone marrow disease over twenty years ago. The doctors told her she would be in a wheelchair. That has not happened, at least not yet.

Knee and Back Surgery

My sister had surgery on both knees and her back. Instead of giving up, she started the foundation Hotels for Children. They go around to hotels where kids stay with no home. They drop off clothes, food vouchers, and odds and ends.

Four-Story Fall

When my cousin was ten years old, he was left at home by himself. Then my uncle got a phone call from the hospital. He was told his son fell out of a four-story building. The reason he fell was he was on the balcony and saw his brother while standing on the banister. He took his hand off to wave. That is when he fell. Not one bone was broken. He had no scratches. He was 100 percent fine and walked away!

Out of Control

A car was out of control. It hit another car going the opposite direction. It pushed the car back. After that, it ran over an adult and child. The back tire ran over the child's spine. The front tire then ran over the child's head. The child jumped up mysteriously. It was like it had never been hit. The child was dragged on the street for about ten feet. Not a scratch. I don't know how it happened.

Near Death

My mom had a near-death experience after a heart attack. She was walking down a white tunnel. At the end was a door. On the other side, she saw her dad and aunt. He told her she needs to go back. He said her kids needed her. At that point, she woke up in the ER from shocks.

Walmart Scammer

I moved to another city and lived with my aunt and her thirty-year-old son. He is not the kind of person you would want to meet. He was very critical and harsh toward me. I was trying to do the right thing. I was trying to better myself. I did not like him. He abuses the system. He gets benefits for kids, which he does not have. He cheated the court and got a minimum-wage job at Walmart to show he makes little money. I was then really depressed. I lost a lot of weight. I then met a friend at Walmart. We became roommates, and everything worked out for a reason.

Holy Spirit

One of the miracles in my life involved a major accident. I was taken to the hospital and underwent hours of surgery. After the surgery, I woke up. I felt the Holy Spirit with me. I felt it protecting me. It taught me, helped me, and led to a deeper faith. I have always been a Christian my whole life. God is saving me for another purpose.

Tooth Pain

I had been suffering from migraine. One night, I went to sleep with a real bad toothache. I had just lost a tooth. About three in the morning, I experienced severe pain in my mouth. My head felt like it was about to burst. My blood pressure went very high. I felt very weak. I thought, *Oh my God, I am going to die.* I went back to sleep, praying to God. I asked for God to please not let anything happen to me. I did not want to die. I still want to see my kids. I was in such severe pain, I could not wake up. As I was praying to God, I had my eyes closed. I felt his presence as he walked in my room. I could not see him physically, nor could I talk to him. He looked at me and walked out. After that, I had no more pain. It was so weird, but it happened to me. So amazing!

Kenny's Story

Here is my story, actually it is my son Kenny's story. He was five years old when we were in a car accident. We were in a fourteen-passenger van. I was picking up kids from school. He asked if he could sit in the back. I said sure. All kids like to sit in the back. He sat down on the passenger side in the back. I said, "Are you buckled?"

He said, "No, wait a minute." He moved over one seat and buckled himself. The impact of the accident happened right where he would have been sitting. He was still seriously injured and broke his right wrist, and his lungs were damaged. He was paralyzed from the neck down. Because the doctors had him incubated, he could not speak or do anything. We were using blinks to communicate.

I would tell him, "Blink once for yes, twice for no."

Then his dad would say, "Blink once for no and twice for yes."

He had many friends. Many wonderful people came and prayed over him. I made a blog on Caring Bridge, and people heard about him. At one point, I had a charismatic healer who wanted to pray over him. I said, "Absolutely, the more, the merrier." He had just had a little taste of chocolate because he could not eat yet. His operation was just finished. He was on a ventilator and could not talk yet, but he wanted a chocolate chip cookie. He could not eat yet, so the healer said, "Kenny, if you want a chocolate chip cookie, I command by the Lord to go ahead and eat it." Also, she said to move his foot. There was no movement in the foot. This was about five weeks after the accident.

We were moving into rehab. I asked the prognosis. The doctor said some people heal completely, others not at all. Kenny is on the lower end. I told him about the healers. He said he thought that was appropriate. He said, "As matter of fact, I think it is appropriate that we pray right now." This was not a church-affiliated hospital, but we held him and prayed for the other four infants that were there. He said, "Dear God, help them to be healed, and help me to do what is best for them to the best of my ability." I always thought that Kenny would regain everything. It has been six years since the accident. He is healing from the outside in. He can move everything, but he is still on a ventilator and in a wheelchair. He can actually stand. It has been slow, like watching your hair grow. There is no brain injury, and he is a strong, willful child. He once asked for a drink at five, and I said, "Use your manners." I asked if he liked to tell people what to do.

He said, "No, Mommy, I love it." He is still quite a character. People have always flocked to him. He has made his own YouTube channel now. He does a little more each day. He updates his improvement to inspire others on YouTube. That was his own idea. In a nutshell, yeah, I have had some miracles in my life.

$40,000 Debt

I was in debt. It totaled about $40,000 dollars. I did not know how I would do it. It was very stressful. Driving one day, I just said, "I am going to give it to God." My CPA called two days later. He said I had a return for $47,000. That was a miracle. I did not know how I would feed my family. It was divine to me.

Parachuting

A man was parachuting. His main chute did not open. Then his backup chute would not open. He fell in a tree and broke every bone in his body. This was a training exercise to go to Vietnam, and every person in his group died in battle. He has bad hearing but is basically alive and well. You never know.

Shot on the Leg

A man was in Vietnam. His whole troop was shot down with a machine gun after leaving the woods. He went out to help and was shot in the leg. The fact he lived is a miracle.

Blood Clots

I was thirty-two and had a hysterectomy. It was supposed to be very simple. However, the surgery was at 6:00 a.m. By 7:30 that night, I started hemorrhaging with blood clots. I had to have another major surgery. I was in the operating room and died. My family said it was the anesthetic. I said, "No, I could remember the pain I felt. I could hear the doctor." All of a sudden, a warm feeling from my toes up encircled me. I felt great. I was in a cocoon. This lasted about thirty seconds. I then heard somebody yell, "I have a heartbeat." I am now sixty-five. I feel I have been living on gravy, and I am doing great.

Midnight Shift

I was going into work. I was called in on the midnight shift. It was a really tough time. My daughter was just diagnosed with cancer. I was driving in the fast lane of the highway. All of a sudden, my car shifted over a lane. I had my hand on the wheel as it changed lanes. I thought my car had lost control. I looked in the left lane and saw a big rig that had totally lost power. I would have slammed in the back of it. It was not me that turned my car. I am night blind anyway. My car saved my life by switching lanes. I told my wife what had happened. I just chalked it up as a memory.

Bookshelf

We were not sure if we were going to keep my daughter. Her chemo had just ended. I asked God, "Please show me a sign if you are here." I had a very secure bookshelf. It opened and slammed the floor. It scared me so bad, I yelled, "Who is in here?" I had a knife in my hand. Then it hit me; there is my sign. I forgot my prayer! I started laughing at the situation. I had asked God to let me know if he was there. I laughed for an hour and could not believe that I was so scared of what I asked for.

Special Lady

While a man was with his girlfriend, a very strange thing happened. A lady came up to him and said how special that lady was. He said thank you. She said, "No, you do not get it. You should stay with this lady forever. I am so serious about this. I do not mean this as a passing compliment." She said, "Look at me in the eyes." He turned to look, and she disappeared. They are happily married now.

Arctic Village

The village I lived in was twenty-three miles above the Arctic circle. There were three thousand people there. I then moved and graduated high school in Anchorage. Then my brother had a liver disease, so we moved to Texas for him to get a transplant. I always wanted to be a professional musician. I never thought it was going to work. I did not think I was good enough. I had two days to practice for an audition for a symphony. I was accepted, which was a miracle to me. My music career has really taken off. I got a teacher that is a world-class musician. That was a miracle. You do not normally get that caliber of teacher. I am currently working on a piece for a competition. If I win, I will be featured as a soloist in the symphony.

Drinking Heavily

I was drinking pretty heavily. One day, I borrowed my dad's truck. I was heading home drunk. I was about two miles from my house. I decided to walk the rest of the way, because I was too drunk. I parked the truck and started walking. Shortly after I started, it started raining. It was a cold rain. I knew it would be a cold and wet walk. I decided to keep going. A made it about fifty feet, and a city bus pulled over. It was not a bus stop. The driver told me to get on. I told him I had no money. He gave me a free ride. Then he dropped me off at my apartment. It was not about money. It was all about compassion.

Mexico

A lady was in Mexico with her husband. They were staying at a hotel. She had a dream that some men were going to come in with bad intentions. She woke up thinking she heard a key in the door. She went back to sleep. She had the dream again. She felt she needed to wake up. When she did, there were three guys in the room staring at her. Her husband got up and yelled. They ran out of the room. It was a miracle that they were not hurt.

Stomach Pains

A lady had severe pains in her stomach for a long period. She did not know what to do. One night, she put a Bible over her stomach. She never had any more stomach pain again.

Diving Board

I was at a swimming pool. A very large lady jumped off a diving board. She saw the other fellow, not Jesus. It was the reaper. We were not allowed to go in the deep end, but I had been sneaking around. I was in the deep end many times. I could swim like a fish. I got her out of the water, as she was not able after the dive. It is instilled in us. God puts his stamp on us. God puts his stamp on everybody, even the mountains and trees. Inanimate objects that we do not know are conscious. God knows, he is the creator.

River

When I was little, my dad took me to the river. I went down, all the way. I saw the whirlpool. Luckily, I had long hair. I am not sure if it was my cousin or someone else. They grabbed my hair and pulled me up to the surface. I am here today!

Train Wreck Nephew

When I was eleven years old, I was in a car accident. We were hit by a train. I was with my nephew. We did not have seatbelts on. One inch front or back, we would have been dragged and killed. I am still here today.

Born In Spite Of

My miracle is I was not supposed to be born. My dad was abusive to my mom for about twenty years. She escaped to a woman's shelter when she was forty. She then found out she was pregnant with me. She was told that it would be a high-risk pregnancy. It would probably be better to have an abortion. Obviously, that did not happen.

Jeep Wreck

I was in a car accident when I was about thirteen. I was hit by a Jeep going sixty miles per hour. I was unconscious for a few days and almost lost my leg and broke several bones. My neighbor was a cop on the scene as well. Though he did not recognize me. I then had a complete recovery.

Dead Man Alive

About seven years ago, something happened. I am a prayer warrior and was at a hospital. There was a young man pronounced dead. The priest had given him his last rights, and the doctor pulled the sheet over his head. They walked out, and we walked in. We prayed with the family. We held hands and laid hands on him. He pulled the sheet back. Needless to say, we continued to pray. My cousin has the gift of healing. She said to the young man, "If you want to live, squeeze my hand." He was over four hundred pounds and has lost a lot of weight. He is still alive today. I know God still performs miracles.

Lupus

I am fifty years old. I was eight when my mother died from lupus. My sister, who will be sixty next month, has lupus. Two of her daughters have the onset of lupus. I was diagnosed with lupus three years ago. It was a Wednesday that I got the call from the doctor. I went to Bible study that night. The pastor was teaching about the woman with the issue of blood. The next day in the afternoon, I called the pastor. I said I wanted to thank him for last night's lecture. I said it was meant for me. He said, "So what is going on?"

I said, "I got a call from the doctor's office."

The pastor then said, "So what does that tell you?"

It is only so if I lack faith. I have not accepted the diagnosis. I said, "I would not receive it." In four months, I went to a specialist. They did more blood work. Then there was no sign of lupus whatsoever.

Phone Mystery

I answered a phone call. Without anything being said, I said my friend's mom just died. That is exactly what happened. Then one day at work, one of my coworkers got a call. I told her my mom just died. I just knew. Kind of weird. I took a little time off to get my composure back. I do not know why I know these things. I just do.

Thanksgiving Trip

It was the day before Thanksgiving. We were traveling in the car. We were going to my grandmother's house. It was my dad and my brother and me. My dad stirred his big soft drink/tea cup. We were on a windy road. He dropped his straw to stir the drink. He reached down and accidently caught the wheel. We hit a curb and tumbled down into a ditch. At that moment, I passed out. My dad proceeded to kick out his side door. He got out and got my brother out. I was trapped in my seatbelt. I could not get out. They had to cut the strap on the seatbelt. Next thing I remember, I woke up and see my mom running down the street. She had just gotten out of the shower. It was less than a mile from my home.

I then felt something on my neck. It was a neck protector. I do not know why, but I did not like it. I was trying to get it off. Then I passed out again. Then I remember waking up. It was all bright around me. I did not know what was going on. I had all these people coming to me. I could see the whole scenario going on. It was like a dream. I witnessed the whole crash, even though I was out. I saw my dad get out and my mom running while I was unconscious.

Lake Light

I was at a lake with my family when I was seven years old. I did not know how to swim. Fear was not a part of me. I decided to go out in the lake. I then started to drown. I was freaking out. Nobody was around. I looked down and saw a light. All of a sudden, I got pulled out. I was traumatized but all right. To this day, I do not know who pulled me out.

Esophagus

I was in the hospital about a year ago. There was a tear in my esophagus. It was a simple procedure. While trying to dilate my esophagus, it tore. I was in ICU for three days. I could not eat and was on morphine. During that time, I was not aware of what was going on. I know that someone was there with me. My hand was being held for a long time. When I opened my eyes, that feeling disappeared. At that moment, I knew that the Lord was with me.

Three and a Half Months

A man was born three and a half months premature. Against all odds, he lived and is healthy.

Gun to Head

I was nearly killed in Vietnam. I got a piece of shrapnel in my leg. I was working as a security guard. I was chasing a guy, and he jumped a fence, and so did I. He was waiting with a gun. He put it on my face. That is when I told him, "Go ahead and take off. This is not worth it." It was not worth a life. He had second thoughts. It was a miracle that he did not kill me. He withdrew the gun and took off running. There were two guys with me waiting at the end.

No Smoke Withdrawal

A lady was a heavy smoker. She had one cigarette left. She was on her way to the bank from her job. She had planned to stop and pick up a pack of cigarettes on the way back. She said it was like God was sitting next to her in the car. He told her to not get another pack. "You are not going to smoke anymore." She quit right then and there. She never had any withdrawal pains. That was years ago.

Twenty-Six-Year-Old Party

My experience happened about eight years ago. I was about twenty-six. I had been at a party. I was doing a lot of drinking and drugs. I was so hopped up on drugs, I ran downtown to the hospital. I collapsed in front of the hospital. At that time, I was an atheist. However, I asked God to save me. When I woke up in the hospital, I was in excruciating pain. I was not aware of my surroundings. I was in the hospital for three months, a third of the time in a coma. I started hallucinating. The room turned black, and objects came out from behind the shadows. It seemed so real. I felt an evil presence. It was like someone was there.

I was in the coma for thirty days. I then kept having dreams. I am not sure if they were dreams or real waking thoughts. I saw a bunch of bad stuff. There were people screaming and crying in darkness. I knew my life was going bad. After leaving the hospital, my wife and I made a commitment to God. I had died in the hospital and had a less than 20 percent chance of survival after being brought back. Regardless of the outcome, my wife decided to go to church every Sunday. She was very scared for obvious reasons. When I got out, my wife kept insisting that I go to church with her. I knew I was in a bad situation.

I recalled black images trying to grab me. There was a lot of torment and pain. I did reach out to God. God was not my Lord and Savior yet; he was just my Creator. At first, I was reluctant. However, I did realize that a power higher than I knew saved me. I started doing some reading and listened to the radio. They were all about spiritual topics. I knew if I died in the hospital, I would have gone to a very bad place. It was dark and black. There were screams and cries with torment and pain. I did not want to go there. I had felt that anguish in the hospital. I knew where my life was heading. I did not want to go back there.

I turned my life completely around. I did a lot of introspection. Now, I am in college. I am going for a doctorate in religious studies. I have seen the light. I want to bring others to heaven as well. Thank God, I got a second chance. Now I know it is my Lord that saved me. I have been through a lot. My death experience was a real eye opener. I saw where I was headed. If I was going to die, that is where I was headed. I do not want that now, or in the future. So I changed my life, and I feel so much better.

Bus Stop

This next miracle came from a guy at a college bus stop. He was about thirty and decided to go back to school. He had been a firefighter. On numerous occasions, he narrowly escaped death. A couple walls fell on him. He was overcome by smoke inhalation and survived. He was shot at several times, thankfully not by marksmen. Many times he brushed with death yet always came out in good shape. He is fine and doing great. We all need to realize that it was not luck. Everything is meant to be.

Thought He Died

He was in a serious car accident. The car rolled over many times. He did not have a seatbelt on. He was ejected out of the car. He thought he had died. He remembers going to heaven. It was an out-of-body experience. He said he was in an intermediary point between earth and heaven. He saw a tunnel and went to a light. He was in a place like a beach area. It was more beautiful than you can imagine. People were congregating almost like tadpoles, like spirits being born. He said he saw Jesus. He was talking to Jesus. He was told, "It is not your time. You need to go back." He did not want to go back. At that point, he was told that someone there needed to talk to him. It was his father. His father gave him a big hug.

He said, "I love you, Dad, and I want to be with you."

He said, "Son, it is not your time to die. You need to go back and tell people what you have seen."

He said, "I do not want to, Father." The father informed him that he did not have a choice. There was an angel there with huge eyes. They looked at each other. Not a word was said. There was a warm glowing feeling. The angel wrapped his arms around him and carried him back. He woke up being resuscitated by the EMS. He had actually died twice. He was a unique individual.

Overcomer

This next story is about surviving and overcoming. Fifteen years ago, a man had bladder cancer. He also had a stroke. He is doing good now, after what would have killed most people.

Alcohol Abuse

(Shotgun in the Mouth)

This is a story of alcohol abuse. A man was sober for one full year. He had been an alcoholic. He went looking for a girl he knew he should not be involved with. He was praying to God, but not Christ. He found himself drinking beer after beer. He had about seven. For some reason, he thought this would help with this girl. He was drunk for a couple days. Kind of lost his mind. He was so destroyed that he just escaped with more beer. He thought he had lost his job. At three or four in the morning, he was up on the edge of his bed. He was going to commit suicide. He put a sawed off shotgun in his mouth.

At that point, the doorbell rang. He yelled, "Who is that?" He was about to shoot the guy at the door. He assumed that it would go from bad to worse, figured the devil was there to claim him. The guy at the door talked him into letting him in. He said, "We had met before." He took the gun as the other man was balling like a baby. That is the day he took Christ as his Lord and Savior.

His bedroom was in the back, with the door shut. Normally, he would not hear the front door. The chance of someone coming at four in the morning was remote. The guy at the door had not seen this man in years. He was a former drug dealer, who now had a ministry. He is a miracle himself. Long story short, he was coming home from a prison ministry. He had gotten really tired. He pulled over and slept for several hours.

When he got to town, he said God told him not to go the usual way. He did not know where he was going. He saw a car with the door open and lights on. That was the suicidal man's car. There were no lights on at the house. He recognized the car from years before. When you are a drunk, you cannot afford a new car. He knocked on the door one second before the other guy blew his head off. He said God sent him to save his life.

Knife

This next story is a reality awakening to the dangers of a knife as told by the victim. I was stabbed when I was a nonbeliever. It hit an artery and nerve and tendon. It was very bad. I was bleeding to death in my front yard. An ambulance happened to be three blocks away. When I closed my eyes, I thought I was dying. The Lord spared me, even though I was not a believer. As a believer, I fell about thirty-two feet. I broke my pelvis and shoulder and fractured my hip. I was falling head first and hit a wall. I did not have surgery; however, I was in a wheelchair for about one year. The first thing I did when I could walk was go door-knocking. I told people that Jesus loves them.

Trials

This is another story of alcohol and drugs. A boy's father figure was a pastor. The pastor died when the boy was seven years old. His real father was an alcoholic and drug user. He was never around. To go to a party was all his father thought about. This went on for five years. The father still was not in the picture. After surviving wrecks and drugs at a later age, just being alive was a miracle. As a man, this guy went through seizures from going cold turkey on alcohol. To add to his serious problems, his four-year-old son was run over and killed by a car. This is just a small sample of the trials that he went through. For fourteen years, he has given his life to Christ and overcome many obstacles.

Snake

A lady was at a seventy-seven-foot cross in Kerrville, Texas—a fascinating place to visit. It is called The Coming King Foundation. She was recalling a miracle in her life. In her words, she said she would like to give a testimony of the power of our Lord Jesus Christ. One evening, she was walking in the dark in her neighborhood. There were no lights, and visibility was very low.

"As I was walking, I heard a soft rattling sound on the asphalt. I looked and could only see a shadow of an oval. I was walking at a good pace. Suddenly, I was walking on the other side of the road. My adrenalin was pumping because I realized I did not jump but was moved. I continued walking home. I felt lifted up, because I knew something had happened. The next day, my neighbor shared an experience she had. As she got out of her car, she saw a rattlesnake. What I heard had to have been a snake. I did not see it. I was miraculously moved. She informed me that that snake was caught and found to be very venomous. Fish and game caught the snake. I know that the Lord moved me or had his angels move me. I never expected anything like that. It was a beautiful circumstance. I praise God for that experience. There was even an article in the paper about this rattlesnake. It was small, but size does not matter with a snake. I praise God in all things."

Bad Meals

This is a story of a man that took medication he was allergic to. His body and kidneys were shutting down. He went to the emergency room at the hospital. At the time, he was very close to death. He was put in a wheelchair and had all the medicine in his body pumped out. He passed out at that point. He had a vision that he was spinning. He was looking up, and air started to come out of a fire sprinkler. He saw a hole open. It was in the sky. There was someone in the hole, but he could not see him. The pressure of the air was blowing him down. He was fighting to get up there. He finally did. He saw blue skies and heaven. Everything was bright and beautiful. Then, a hand pulled him down. He woke up three days later in the intensive care unit. It was a miracle he survived as well as his vision.

Wyoming Accident

An auto accident happened after a major snowstorm. Four people were going south out of Wyoming. The vehicle lost control and flipped. One person was injured. A broken neck and pelvis. The other three were not injured in any way. The injured person healed after a time. It was a miracle they all were not killed.

Doctor-Guided

The following is from a very religious man. He said God put us here to help each other. His sister-in-law had seizures frequently. He did not know what it was when she had one. He called 911. The ambulance arrived quickly and rushed her to the hospital. After arriving at the hospital, she had repeating seizures. The doctor examined her brain. He did not see anything unusual. The doctor said, "I know just the cure for her." He added this to the IV. She woke up from a sleep.

She inquired, "What am I doing here?" She said, "I want to go home." What the Lord can do is a miracle. I think that was a miracle. With the Lord's help and guidance for the doctor, she was fine.

Horrific Wreck

This is a story of survival of a horrific car accident. My mother-in-law was hit head-on by a drunk driver. It was so bad, the emergency brake went through her fibula. When the ambulance got there, they had to cut the emergency brake away. She said when this was all happening, she felt a gentle pull. She later said they were angels.

Leukemia Survivor

The following miracle came from a lady in an amusement park. Her daughter had leukemia. She had two bone marrow transplants. She was given a 10 percent survival chance. That was seventeen years ago. She is now a teacher. She is doing well. Her daughter is a miracle, and she thanks the Lord every day that she has her in her life.

CPR

This is a story of how a wife saved her husband three times.

"The first time, I was sitting in a recliner. My feet were higher than my head. I had stopped my breathing. I turned blue. My wife gave me CPR and called 911. The second time, I do not recall, other than waking up in the ambulance. She had given me CPR again and called 911. The third time, she could not wake me up. I had stopped breathing. I woke up with a tube in my nose. That really scared me. I am going to Virginia to have a sleep study done. I need to figure out what is going on."

Coffee Pot

When I was two years old, my mother got a new coffee pot. She had just gotten it for Christmas from my aunt. It was one of those old percolators. The top screw came out and flipped onto my body. It burned over 90 percent of my body. They were third-degree burns. She took me to the hospital. They said, "Take him home and let him die. There is no way we can save him." She took me over to Virginia where my dad was in the army and accepted it.

It took two years, but I recovered. Sometimes, doctors do not know.

Parkinson

I had cancer when I was thirty-nine years old. I prayed to the Lord and overcame. I started running. At first I could barely make it around the block. Within the first year, I ran my first marathon. Within a few years, I ran in four more. I ran in Paris, France. I now have Parkinson's disease. It was about two years ago that I was diagnosed. I bought a bike and started riding. At first, I could only go about two miles. I worked up to forty miles. My doctor said, "You are sixty-three and can do more than my twenty-five-year-old son." He took me off all medication. The bottom line is, I was blessed. I am not sure I have kicked it, but I have been off medication for a year. Through physical activity and the grace of the Lord, I have been able to thrive.

$500

My sister had gotten sick. We took her to the hospital. The medicine she needed was worth $500. My dad used our rent money to pay for the medication. After leaving the hospital, we headed home. In the driveway was $500. To say we were thankful is an understatement.

Birth

Child birth is something we take for granted. My wife had two miscarriages and became pregnant again. We were very concerned that it could be a third time. Anyway, I now have a healthy four-year-old girl. She is our miracle from God.

Tunnel

This next miracle cannot be explained logically. When a man was eleven years old, he got run over by a bus leaving school. It destroyed all of his body. He remembered that he died. He remembered going through a tunnel. At the end of the tunnel, a voice called him. It said, "Come on, come on, come on". Then he turned and heard his mom's voice.

She told him, "Don't go, come back."

The voice in the tunnel said, "Go back." The next thing he knew, he opened his eyes in the hospital.

White Star

I was at a camp on a church retreat. I was going through a rough time. One night when I was going to bed, a dark shadow was on the side of the bed. I started praying. All I saw after that was a white star. I saw it every night. I knew someone was watching over me.

Against All Odds

The power of love is not measurable. It can cause things to happen. About two years ago, a young man was a missionary in Ghana, West Africa. His grandfather became very ill in the States. Through e-mail, the grandson was informed his grandfather was in the hospital and had not eaten for three days. He suffered from Alzheimer's disease for five years. The doctors said that he was about to die. They said his brain was not functioning. He could not even hold a fork.

After returning home, the young man insisted that the first thing he did was see his grandpa. We drove to see him. Disbelief was overwhelming for the young man. His grandfather was hooked up to an oxygen machine. As his will stated, he did not want a feeding tube. Blood was being pumped into him. That is the only way he survived. The nurses always brought mashed potatoes and meatloaf every day.

Then, a strange thing happened. He asked if there were mashed potatoes. The nurse said, "Are you hungry?"

He said, "Yes, I feel like I haven't eaten in days." Three days later, the doctor said there was nothing more they could do for him. They decided to pump extra blood in him and take him home. The doctor advised him to notify the family and next of kin. He notified a lot of people. The young man was in another room, ordering food. The doctor came in and said that his grandpa had started speaking. This was the first words in a week. He also grabbed a fork and fed himself. This was part of the mashed potato incident. After being taken home, he improved dramatically. In less than three months, he started walking. The doctor said he would never walk again, but even the doctor could not explain what happened. There was always Christian music playing in the hospital room and at home. The power of God was at work. He walked for eight months before a broken ankle made him bedridden.

Fed Ex Rain

I n one such experience, I was driving in an early rain on Highway 240 in Memphis, Tennessee, headed to work at the FedEx hub during rush hour traffic. Due to the slick state of the road, I was forced into the left emergency lane by a fishtailing vehicle in front of me. I quickly realized the reason for the fishtailing vehicles actions: in the emergency lane, another vehicle was parked sideways, having collided head on into the central median. I was unable to exit the emergency lane as the driver of the fishtailing vehicle righted himself as I came alongside him. I consequently rammed into the wrecked vehicle. I can see the entire event unfold in my memory to this day.

My front right tire locked up as a result of the impact, which jolted my vehicle hard to the right. I very quickly raced across all three lanes of rush hour traffic at a near perpendicular slant, yet my vehicle came to rest on the far right side lawn, unscathed, save for the single original collision that vaulted my vehicle to its resting place. While the vehicle would eventually be determined a total loss, I exited the spent vehicle with nary a scratch, no worse for wear. I believe the fact I was not even slightly hurt, not from the fishtailing vehicle nor the singular collision nor the uncontrolled and sudden crossing of the three-lane highway in less than ideal road conditions nor going off the road and coming to rest on the far right embankment is no small miracle.

Right Through

A very good friend of the author, who is of the highest integrity, told this story about his mom. She was driving and approached a traffic signal. It was green, and she proceeded along. A pickup going the other direction ran a red light at high speed. She got ready to die as it was coming right at her. The truck went right through her vehicle. There was no physical contact. Please consider to doubt this is to limit the unlimited! That lady is very involved in a large church. It was not her time.

Stomach Pains

Back in 2009, I was having stomach pains. I was not too sure what was going on. I told my husband about it. He just said stay at home as we had no health insurance. So, I stayed home. My stomach pain got worse. It got to the point that I could not even stand up. When I tried, I would fall down. It was so bad, I went to the hospital emergency room. The hospital admitted me. They found out I had a ruptured fallopian tube. Those are the tubes that carry the egg from the ovary to the uterus. I had been bleeding internally for two weeks. The doctor that could do the procedure was at the hospital. He was the only one who could do it. He saved my life. I would have died from lack of blood. He was able to do the surgery.

80 M.P.H.

A man and his friend had a wreck on the freeway. They were going eighty miles per hour and very drunk. They ran into a car in a serious accident. The officer came up to the driver later and said, "Who are you guys?" They said we were in this car. He said, "You must have been in the backseat.

He said, "No, sir, we were in the front seat."

The officer said, "That is impossible. The two guys in the front were killed."

Gift Of Love

I was baptized in a lake. I heard a voice say, "Let go of all your sins and everyone else's." When I came up, the sky caught on fire in my mind. A few days later, I got a card. It said, "A gift is not something you buy, it is not a trophy, it is not something you work hard for, it is something that is simply given to you. A child can accept this gift, an adult can except this gift. The gift is love from God."

If you are inspired to share a miracle, please send to dccobb111@ gmail.com

Thank You

About the Author

Tabor Hermon is a sixty-one year old. About six feet, three inches and two hundred pounds. He plays guitar and sings—not subject to what people think, just God. He walks very frequently and is an avid reader. He talks about politics and religion and does not wonder why there are arguments. "You do not have to agree with someone to love them. If that were the case, God would not love us." He enjoys nature very much, in wonder of it all. Water is an unusual attraction and perhaps he should have been a fish. He is a vegetarian for seventeen years (not judgmental). "Live and let live, although that does not fly." He enjoys classic rock music with clean, positive lyrics. He plays in nursing homes and assisted living facilities and is still learning more every day. He will never stop. If only one-tenth of past could be remembered. He is not fond of the saying that "If I had it all to do over again, I would not change a thing." He would change thousands. Many miracles in the book involve the author. He is thankful for everything. He feels love is the answer.

CPSIA information can be obtained
at www.ICGtesting.com
Printed in the USA
LVOW07s2344290717
543089LV00001BA/1/P